RIDING
TECHNIQUES

FOREWORD BY TINA SEDERHOLM

YOUR HORSE
MAGAZINE

RIDING
TECHNIQUES

FOREWORD BY TINA SEDERHOLM

YOUR
HORSE
MAGAZINE

First published in 2003

A catalogue record for this book is available from the British Library

ISBN 1 84425 089 X

Published jointly by
Haynes Publishing, Sparkford,
Yeovil, Somerset BA22 7JJ, England
Phone 01963 440635, www.haynes.co.uk
And
Emap Active Limited,
Wentworth House, Wentworth Street,
Peterborough PE1 1DS, England
Phone 01733 213700, www.emap.com

Produced for Haynes Publishing and Emap Active Ltd by
PAGEOne, 5 Missenden Road, Chesham, Bucks HP5 1JL, England

Printed and bound in England by J.H. Haynes & Co. Ltd, Sparkford

Contents

Photography by **Matthew Roberts**

Foreword

The desire in human beings to improve is a strong one. Talk to most riders and you will discover they are pursuing one goal or another – wanting to jump higher, wider, faster. Sometimes the goal is to overcome a fear. What is common to all these ambitions is a desire to make the most of what we have and who we are. The burning question is, how do I do that?

As you have picked up this book, you may well be asking yourself that very question. In it you will find a collection of articles on riding and training horses, featuring trainers from many branches of equestrianism. Some are top competitors, such as Peter Charles in show jumping, Matt Ryan and Karen Dixon in Horse Trials and Joanna Jackson from the world of dressage. Others are those who have devoted more of their lives to full time training, and have gathered their knowledge from a variety of sources, including techniques from outside the horse world, in order to advance equestrian education.

The advice in this book falls into three categories. Some of it is general – covering overall philosophies and approaches to riding, fitness and competing. The last section, which features many of my own articles, deals with specific problems and provides tailor made exercises to overcome those challenges. The first section includes the 'private lessons', in which you can get an insight into the way particular combinations make progress and deal with common issues.

As you read this book, you will see some common themes emerging. Most obviously, the trainers featured here put the onus of education onto the rider. There is a saying – "A horse is always a horse, but a human being is not always a rider." Without exception, the trainers in this book start by focussing their attention on the rider's position and the correct application of the aids. For if the rider is not giving clear messages, how can he expect the horse to respond satisfactorily?

Examining the way he or she is communicating with the horse is an ongoing process for any rider, throughout their career. Many of the frustrations I encounter in my own students stem from them either unconsciously blocking the horse in some way, or by giving the horse confusing aids. I myself have done this more times than I care to remember.

Of course, horses also need to be educated, and again you will see a similarity in the underlying themes that emerge from these articles. The trainers focus on one or more of the following principles: the importance of the horse responding to forward and collecting aids, and that the horse is in a good balance and rhythm. They also promote the significance of making the horse supple, and the vital work on straightness, and pay attention to creating focus and confidence in both horse and rider. I consider these to be the ground rules for training horses, and all effective schooling and jumping exercises are designed around educating and improving horses in these areas.

The horses' education, particularly at the beginning of his life, needs to be done by a knowledgeable and sympathetic horseman. It takes longer than riders sometimes think to become the type of rider who is capable of giving the horse a good start.

It is not only young horses that benefit from a good start. If you, as a rider, are at the beginning of your learning curve, find yourself a positive, knowledgeable and enthusiastic horseman or woman to teach you. Nearly all the top riders I know point to a significant mentor in their early riding years.

I was lucky enough to grow up at an international training centre. My father, who was my main teacher, was Olympic trainer to four different nations, and our training centre catered for more than three hundred pupils and four hundred horses a year. However, even in these unique circumstances, I still had to go through many processes of trial and error, making mistakes, falling off, messing up, learning solutions, and then being faced with a new challenge. It is likely that you will go through a similar process in your own riding career. The key is to use problems and setbacks to your advantage. Ask yourself, what lesson is there for me in this situation? The answers you get will provide you with your next steps, and will turn a problem into something useful.

In my opinion, gaining a thorough knowledge of the basics of riding and horsemanship generally means sticking with one trainer or school of thought for a certain length of time. I have found that riders who skip from one trainer to another too early on often end up confused from an overdose of information. However, once a rider has a solid foundation, it then becomes valuable to gather knowledge from other sources. Hearing an old idea expressed in a new way can bring about a big change.

As you study this book more closely, you may discover one other, initially confusing, factor. The trainers here, although linked with a common aim of getting the most out of horses and improving the relationship between horses and riders, vary in their methodology, particularly if they are oriented towards different sports. To this paradox, I would say this: There is a danger in looking for the definitive answer to riding and training horses. There is often more than one route to getting a certain result. In the end, the best instructors and riders in the world are the ones who are constantly open to new learning.

Eventually you will discover that your horses are your best teachers. The best you can do is take the suggestions in this book, try them out and see which ones work for you. You can guarantee that your horse will give you feedback about your actions. The trick is first to notice the feedback, and then learn how to interpret it.

Above all, enjoy the journey of creating a long-lasting and successful partnership with your horse. Always remember the reason that you first got involved with horses. For me, it was because I love then and was in awe of what a horse and rider could do together. Combine that with a desire to keep learning and your life with horses will be an interesting and stimulating one.

Tina Sederholm
JUNE 2003

Private Lessons

THE TRAINERS

Jeanette Brakewell is an Olympic three–day event rider. She was part of the silver medal–winning team at the Sydney 2000 Olympics. Jeanette had two horses in the top 10 at Burghley Horse Trials in 2002 and won an individual silver medal at the World Equestrian Games in Jerez.

Irish rider **Peter Charles** is a top international show jumper. He is based in Hampshire and divides his time between training horses and competing all over the world. His many wins include both the 2001 Hickstead Derby competitions.

Three–day event rider **Karen Dixon** has represented Britain at four Olympic Games – Seoul, Barcelona, Atlanta and Sydney. One of the country's most successful riders, Karen is based in County Durham and divides her time between training her string of top horses and teaching.

Joanna Jackson is an international dressage rider and trainer. She has been a member of British dressage teams at young rider and senior levels. Joanna represented Great Britain at the 1996 Atlanta Olympics with Mester Mouse. She is currently based in Gloucestershire where she trains horses and riders..

Mia Korenika BHSII is a show jumper and trainer. Mia represented Britain in the under–21s show jumping team in 1990 and 1991 and now runs a livery/training yard in Northamptonshire. She competes regularly.

Show jumper **Geoff Luckett** is well known on the international circuit as one of the UK's top riders and trainers. He's been a member of Britain's Nations Cup team a total of eight times and is a regular at world–class shows with his leading horses Broadstone Lady's Man and Antoinette II.

Chris McGrann is based in Yorkshire where he trains riders of all levels. One of his most successful former pupils is Olympic silver medallist Jeanette Brakewell. He is a Riding Club Master Judge and a member of The Pony Club training committee.

Angela Niemeyer Eastwood is a dressage rider and trainer. She has competed in 3DEs but now concentrates on dressage and runs Knights End Farm, a training, competition and livery yard in Cambridgeshire.

Triple Olympic gold medallist **Matt Ryan** is one of the world's greatest three–day eventers. A member of Australia's gold medal winning team at the Sydney Olympics in 2000, he came 15th at Burghley in 2001 riding his Olympic horse, Kibah Sandstone. For more on Matt, visit his website – www.mattryan.co.uk

Tina Sederholm has been involved in training horses and riders from novice to Olympic standard for the last 15 years. Tina's parents ran an internationally renowned training centre. She has competed regularly at Advanced level – including three–day events such as Blenheim, Bramham and Windsor.

Prepare for take-off

Problem: Your horse is a talented jumper, but he can stop without warning, leaving you in mid air – or on the floor!

Trainer: Peter Charles

Falling off knocks your confidence, but confidence is vital if you and your horse are both going to enjoy your jumping. When you know your horse isn't as committed to jumping a fence as you are, it can be a vicious circle. As you approach the jump with your heart in your mouth, self-preservation tells you to fear the worst so you'll be ready for anything that happens. But you know you have to be positive or your horse will sense your nerves.

If your horse is an inconsistent jumper it may be because he's lacking in confidence. Worry can cause him to rush into fences or stop.

With careful riding you can give your horse confidence. If you can help him to settle into a good rhythm and get him to relax, he will find jumping a lot easier and more enjoyable.

If your horse isn't as keen on jumping as you'd like him to be, it's all too easy to overcompensate and try too hard to get him over the fence – especially if you're anticipating a stop. This leaves you doing all the work. It also makes it more difficult for your horse to find his natural rhythm and balance.

When you run into problems with your jumping, some expert advice can make a big difference to your performance.

Sue Ritchie has owned 15.2hh, seven–year-old TBx, Tarran Lad since he was three. The pair compete in Prelim dressage and riding club events. Sue enjoys show jumping but Tarran Lad often has other ideas – he can be spooky and putting in sudden stops is his speciality. As a result, Sue tends to hit the deck!

Not surprisingly, Sue would like to make falling off a less regular occurrence, so the aim of today's lesson is to work on improving her position and jumping technique. This will help Sue to be more secure in the saddle and will give her and Tarran Lad more confidence in their jumping.

The lesson

GETTING STARTED

Peter watches Sue as she warms up. Tarran Lad has a quick walk and she finds it difficult to keep him at a slower pace. Peter notices that Sue tends to have her reins a little too long and she allows her elbows to stick out (pic above). He suggests that shortening her reins slightly, and working on keeping her elbows by her sides, will give her more control.

Peter comments that Sue's seat and leg position is good. He reminds her to keep her weight pushed firmly down into her heels. This will help to stop her lower leg from swinging, especially in canter.

> **Peter's tip**
>
> ■ Shortening your stirrups helps to improve your seat. Peter explains that this tenses the thighs which helps push your weight into your seat. This makes you more secure and helps you absorb your horse's movement.

Private Lessons

ONE JUMP AHEAD

Peter sets up a small cross-pole for Sue and Tarran Lad to jump so he can assess what they need to work on. He notices that they take off with a long stride, too far away from the jump. Peter thinks Sue is having trouble because she's coming in to the jump too fast and having a bit of a panic at the last minute. He also notices that, in her anticipation of the jump, Sue tends to move forward into jumping position too soon. "If the horse was to stop, you'd have no chance because you're in front of the movement," Peter warns.

Peter's tip

■ If you struggle with canter strike–offs, Peter has an exercise to help you get them right every time.

When you're asking for canter it's easy to lose your balance, tip forward and dip into the transition.

Often you need to do the opposite of what you might think. For example, to get left canter you have to be strong with your right side. Practise this on a circle. Keep your weight to the right, use your right leg, keep your right rein, but maintain the left bend and, most importantly, don't look down.

GENTLY DOES IT

Peter tells Sue she must think steady on the approach. "Don't push into the fence, keep your body still and let the horse come to the jump. Don't try to jump it before he does, and don't be tempted to move your upper body until he takes off," he says.

Peter explains that if Sue can get Tarran Lad closer to the fence, he will be more likely to jump it. "It's much easier for the horse if he takes off in the right place," he tells her.

Peter says that Sue will find it very difficult to progress with her jumping unless she can break the habit of taking a long, kicking stride into her fences (pic left). Once she can do this, it will give her and her horse a lot more confidence and the risk of stopping will disappear.

Sue needs to be sitting more in the saddle as she approaches the fence (pic left), so it's easier for her to hold the canter together.

Peter works on helping Sue to slow down the canter and shorten Tarran Lad's stride with transitions and circles. He reminds her that, even though she wants to slow the stride, she should keep her leg on so the canter does not become long and flat.

Peter's tip

■ When you're building a horse's confidence, jump him over small, single fences. Don't ask too much of him and remember to praise him when he gets it right.

Peter's tip

■ To test your control, see how well you can lengthen and shorten your horse's canter strides. This helps you to get your horse really listening to you and will improve the quality of the pace. Don't mistake speed for lengthening – your horse should take bigger steps but the rhythm should stay the same.

WAITING GAME

Sue tends to fire Tarran Lad at the fences. She should sit quietly on the approach and keep the contact. Peter tells her to wait for the extra stride that Tarran Lad usually misses before a fence. To make their jumping more consistent, Sue must try to slow down the approach.

After a few attempts putting Peter's advice into practice, Sue approaches the fence much more calmly. Now she's not in front of the movement, She manages to shorten Tarran Lad's stride and get him closer to the fence before he takes off.

Peter notices that Sue sometimes looks down as she jumps (pic below). He points out that this can be a big mistake. "If anything goes wrong and you're looking down, you'll go over the handlebars because you're naturally going that way," he explains.

Peter's tip

■ Tarran Lad can get nappy: he plants his feet firmly and refuses to go forward. Peter gives Sue an easy way to get him going again without having an argument. "When he gets stroppy, just turn him onto a small circle. Doing this takes him off balance so he has to step forward. Then you can gradually make your circle bigger," he says.

Peter explains that this nappiness can be overcome with practice but only if you have a system. "You won't win if you try to get him forward on a straight line," he says.

Sue tries the fence again. "Come quietly into it and give yourself time," Peter reminds her. This time it's perfect and the canter is more composed. Peter points out that this control gives Sue a few more gears on her approach. He explains that holding, then firing, the horse into a fence doesn't work, it just makes the jumping erratic.

THE VERDICT

Peter and Sue are pleased with today's progress. Tarran Lad has jumped really well and not put in any nasty stops.

Although it's tempting to carry on, Peter feels it's a good idea to finish on a good note. "To do any more would be greedy," he says. "Horses can get nappy if you keep on asking for more. It's best to stop while their confidence is high, rather than risk them getting sour."

Peter doesn't think the pair will have any trouble improving their jumping. "All they need is practice. If Sue can work on getting the basics right, working on the rhythm and approach to small fences, they should be able to tackle 3'-3'6" courses no problem.

"At the end of the lesson Sue's position is much more secure. If she can keep it that way she won't be having any more trips to casualty!"

Homework

Building their confidence is vital for Sue and Tarran Lad and Peter says it's important that they don't try to jump too big initially.

It's difficult to break old habits, so Sue will need to practise her jumping, working on maintaining a steady, calm rhythm.

Sue must resist the temptation to move her body forward until the horse leaves the ground. If she does this and remembers to look ahead over the fence, her position will become more secure and it will help her to stay in the saddle if Tarran Lad stops.

Problem: Your horse is still a baby, he hasn't done much and you're keen to get started on some dressage but you need to teach him lengthened strides.

Trainer: Joanna Jackson

Learning to lengthen

Everyone has to start somewhere. Even top-level competition horses were once novices with a lifetime of learning ahead of them.

Lengthened strides is one of the movements that novice dressage horses are expected to perform. The exercise is used as preparation for medium and extended paces which come later in the horse's training. The judge is looking to see that the horse is accepting the rider's aids by taking bigger, not faster steps, while keeping the rhythm and balance of his trot.

To give a young horse the best start in life, the foundations of his training need to be correct from the beginning. Even when you're teaching your horse the smallest things, it's important to get them right. This will make everything you do with him in the future easier and more successful.

Learning any dressage movement takes practice and know how, especially if you or your horse haven't done it before. Knowing where to start can be difficult, that's why getting a few tricks of the trade from an expert can make all the difference.

Victoria Aston has owned Wilson a 15.3hh Dutch Warmblood for six months. Wilson is four years old and Victoria is about to take him to his first affiliated dressage competition. Victoria also hopes to do some show jumping with Wilson but, for the moment, she wants to concentrate on their dressage.

Wilson is showing a real talent for dressage, but before Victoria can do any novice tests on him she needs to teach him lengthened strides. Victoria thinks Wilson's main problem is that he can be a bit lazy, so he's struggling with lengthening. The aim of today's lesson is to give her some tips on lengthening that will help with his training.

The lesson
ONE STEP AT A TIME

The aim of working your horse deep is to get him to stretch down until his mouth is at least level with his elbows

Before Victoria can ask for lengthened strides, she needs to get Wilson properly warmed up. Joanna says: "Start by working him deep, this will help you to remove any tension in his body and get him soft and relaxed," she says.

Joanna suggests that Victoria gives Wilson a canter. She explains that this will help to liven him up and get him in a more forward-thinking mood. This will make it easier for her when she asks for lengthening.

Joanna's tip

■ Working your horse deep is a good suppling exercise. To do it, gradually give the reins to encourage your horse to stretch his neck forwards and down. You don't want him to get on his forehand, so remember to keep your leg on so his hindquarters stay active. If your horse is working correctly he should be able to keep his rhythm and balance. If there is tension in his neck and back he'll find it more difficult to stretch down.

Private Lessons

ONE STEP AT A TIME

Getting a good canter transition every time can be difficult with a young horse

Wilson is young and he can get a little unbalanced at times so it's important for Victoria to give him some help. Joanna sees that Wilson's transitions into canter aren't always smooth and he tends to fling himself into them (pic above). Joanna tells Victoria she will get a better transition if she makes sure the trot has a good rhythm first. It will also be easier for Wilson to pick up the canter if he is correctly bent to the inside. Joanna explains that asking for canter on a circle will make it easier for her to keep everything more together.

Joanna points out that it's important not to get into the habit of holding the horse in place with the contact. "Use little half-halts and give your inside rein occasionally, just to keep him loose and soft, rather than allowing him to get set in his neck," she says.

Wilson's canter is getting a little bit hurried so Joanna reminds Victoria to sit on her bottom and push her hips forward. "Think of having your shoulders behind your hips," she says.

Joanna explains to Victoria that keeping her weight in the saddle will help her to get Wilson to take more weight off his forehand and encourage him to use his hindlegs with more power (pic right).

Joanna's tip

■ Be careful not to confuse impulsion with speed. It's a common mistake to make, especially when you're riding a test. When you're asking your horse to be more energetic, think of containing that energy rather than letting it all speed away.

This time the canter transition is much better

Lengthening on a circle can be a useful exercise

A LENGTHY ISSUE

Now Wilson is ready to start doing some lengthening. Joanna asks Victoria to trot him on a 20m circle (pic above). She explains that staying on a circle helps to keep the energy and impulsion. "Use your legs together to ask him to lengthen his stride and cover more ground," Joanna says. "Ask with your legs in the rhythm of the trot. Then, once he's lengthening, be ready to adjust your aids."

Victoria must allow Wilson to stretch his neck but she mustn't let the reins get too long. "Think of keeping the bit in the corners of his mouth," Joanna says. "If you hold your reins slightly out to the sides, with your hands wider apart, it helps you to keep the contact," she adds (pic far right).

Victoria has a lot to think about and Joanna reminds her to be conscious of her upper body. "It's important to try to sit up so you're not putting all your weight over the horse's shoulders,"

Remember to give your horse chance to rest during your schooling sessions

she says.

Wilson is really trying. "He's being very good and it's hard work," says Joanna. She tells Victoria to let him have a little stretch and a breather before they do any more (pic above).

Joanna's tip

■ Holding your hands out to the sides can be a useful exercise, especially with a younger horse. It makes it easier for you to maintain the contact and also helps the horse with his balance. It is particularly useful when you're asking more from the horse with your legs, otherwise he can feel restricted – rather like you've got the handbrake on.

Private
Lessons

Developing a nice balanced, bouncy canter will improve your trot work

AIDS FOR LENGTHENING

Before you ask for lengthened strides, make sure you have a good quality trot. It should be nice and powerful and free from any tension. Prepare your horse for the transition with a half-halt, this gets him listening to you and encourages him to really activate his hindlegs.

Then you need to use your weight and both your legs smoothly and at the same time, to push the horse forward and encourage him to take longer steps. The rein contact should not be affected, but be ready to give with your hands as the horse stretches and lengthens his frame.

Homework

Wilson is only four and Joanna says he is progressing really well with his training. He's getting the hang of lengthened strides and they will improve as he gets more experience and practice.

When Victoria works on lengthening it's important she remembers to make a big fuss of Wilson when he tries hard and gets it right, even if it's just a couple of strides.

Joanna explains that if he's made to feel clever and good about himself, he'll be more generous and willing to try next time he's asked to repeat the exercise.

PRACTICE MAKES PERFECT

Another way to practise lengthened strides is to do it down the long side of the arena. Joanna warns Victoria that she will have to be careful when she does this as it's easier for the horse to get long and flat in his outline when he's not lengthening on the circle.

"Prepare by riding a circle and get a good active trot first. When you're happy with the trot, ride down the long side and ask for some lengthening. Give him a little tap with your whip if necessary," she says.

Joanna explains that when a horse is still learning to do lengthened strides and doesn't quite understand, you may have to let him run faster into it a little, just until he gets braver. "As soon as you feel him take a couple of longer steps, bring him back and reward him so he gets the idea," she says.

"When you're pushing the horse forward you need to be careful that all the energy doesn't run out the front door," Joanna warns, "It helps if you don't let your reins get too long."

Riding a few transitions helps to keep the trot active and relaxed. Joanna gets Victoria to break up their lengthening work by practising some more canter transitions.

"If you can work on improving Wilson's balance in the canter transitions, it will help his balance in the lengthening," she says. Joanna explains that everything in a horse's training is connected. "If he's capable of using his hindlegs to power his body into canter, he is capable of using them to take longer steps."

THE VERDICT

Wilson has tried really hard and Joanna and Victoria are pleased with his progress. "It's important not to do too much with him at this stage, a few lengthened strides are enough," Joanna says.

Joanna thinks Wilson has lovely paces and he should do well at dressage. She says Victoria is doing a good job of training him and she just has to work on keeping him active and balanced.

Victoria has got some useful tips from the lesson that should help her with Wilson's training and prepare them for some good dressage tests in the future.

When you're starting to teach your horse lengthened strides, be happy with just one or two steps to begin with

Private Lessons

Gael-Ann Clancy is a part-time riding instructor and has owned 16.2hh, six-year-old Shire x TB Beth for six months. Gael-Ann has done a lot of show jumping but Beth is new to the sport, having competed in a few unafilliated classes.

Beth is a typical youngster and, as a result, her concentration can fail her. Gael-Ann would like to improve Beth's technique and teach her to focus on the fence in hand.

The young ones

Problem: You have a lot of show jumping experience but your horse is young and lacks concentration.

Trainer: Geoff Luckett

Teaching a young horse to show jump can be tricky. It may be natural for a horse to jump, but trying to teach a youngster that it's a good idea to slow down, concentrate, round over the fence and tackle all types and colours of jump is a different matter.

It takes time, patience and skill to train an inexperienced horse and it's a good idea to keep each step as simple as possible. Start with plenty of poles on the ground and grid-style fences to teach the horse to concentrate.

It helps to have an expert eye on the ground to iron out any problems and keep you on track, so arrange to have some lessons to give you both confidence and advice.

The lesson

WARMING UP

As Gael-Ann and Beth warm up on the flat, Geoff advises Gael-Ann to take a bit of weight out of the saddle rather than sitting deep. She also needs to shorten her reins slightly to ask Beth to come together as the horse tends to dictate the pace.

Geoff reminds Gael-Ann to avoid trotting when jumping and go straight from walk to canter and vice versa. This way, the horse gets used to always cantering at a jump, which will make jumping a lot easier, and he is less likely to drop down into trot if the rider forgets to push on.

"The horse should carry on cantering, even if you are not concentrating 100%" says Geoff. "Drill it into the horse's mind that everything is done from a canter."

JUMP TO IT

The first jump of the day is a simple cross-pole. Beth tends to rush her fences, a common problem in young horses, and at first Gael-Ann struggles to find the right stride. "Don't waste time looking for a stride," Geoff explains, "Just ask for a nice short canter and let the horse come into the fence and jump it. The most important thing is that the horse jumps in a rhythm. Instead of looking for a stride, keep the pace bouncy and hold the horse together."

Gael-Ann and Beth jump clear each time, but it's obvious that Gael-Ann feels the need to push on and do all the work. She's convinced that, if she doesn't push, Beth will slip into trot – which makes it hard work. Instead, Geoff advises her to work on maintaining a nice, bouncy canter which will naturally carry them over the fences.

To get a feel for how Beth moves, Geoff jumps on and is surprised at how spongy her movements are – there's no real sense of direction or control. He suggests Gael-Ann works on the flat to improve her co-ordination and steering.

Beth has a good, natural jump and is happy as long as things are going her way. But Geoff notices that she has no real discipline and this is something else Gael-Ann will have to work on if she wants their jumping to improve. "Your throttle and your brakes should be spot on," says Geoff. "So work on this on the flat and you'll be much more in control."

AT THE DOUBLE

As Geoff sets up a simple double – two cross-poles with a pole on the ground in between –Beth shows her nappy side. They jump it clear but Beth almost refuses the second part and Gael-Ann has to really kick on to get her over. Unsettled, Beth then rushes over the double the second time, so Geoff asks Gael-Ann to work on the flat with plenty of canter circles to slow down Beth and get her concentrating on the rider.

THREE'S A CROWD

Gael-Ann jumps the double a couple more times, and when Geoff adds a third cross-pole to make a triple, the pair jump it clear. However, Beth is still rushing and flattening over the fences. At this height, she gets away with it, but Gael-Ann will have to spend lots of time getting her to shorten up and stay in a rhythm if she wants to tackle bigger, more technical courses.

After jumping the triple clear twice however, things start to go wrong. At the third attempt Beth clips the middle jump and by the fourth try she's starting to stare over at the other horses on the yard rather than concentrate on the approach. Beth naps coming round the corner towards the first fence and her concentration has evaporated. She rushes the triple and flattens the last fence, so Geoff takes the reins again.

As Geoff works Beth on the flat, concentrating on getting a steady, collected canter, he's working on getting her to focus on what he's telling her to do and listen. Geoff jumps a now far more collected Beth over the triple and it's less rushed, so this is something Gael-Ann needs to work on.

Geoff's tip

■ "Don't just sit there waiting for the horse to jump," says Geoff, "Sit up, keep the horse up on the bridle and ride him over. You want him so together and bouncy you could imagine he's almost sitting on his haunches."

Homework

Gael-Ann needs to work Beth on the flat – with lunge and ridden work – to get her listening more.

She also needs to aim for a collected, bouncy, effortless canter, so that Beth gets into a natural rhythm – and sticks to it while she's jumping. If Beth lapses into trot, they should stop and go straight into canter again – no trotting is allowed! Gael-Ann should also lift her reins and get up out of the saddle more.

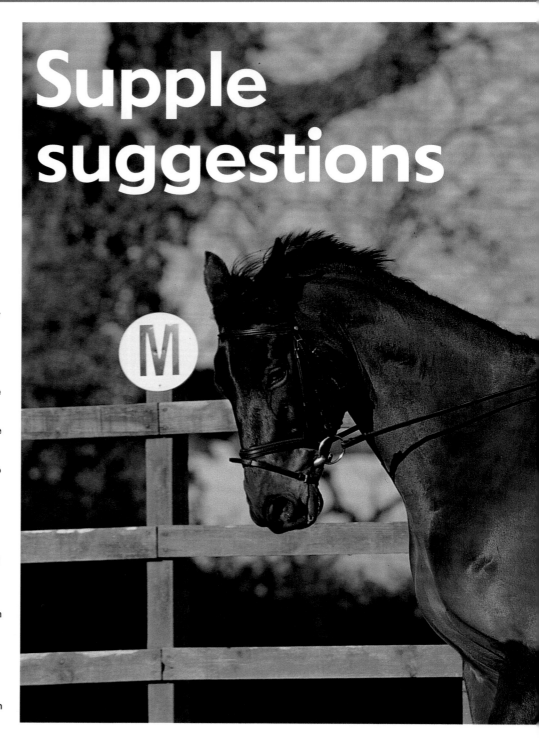

Supple suggestions

Problem: Your horse has potential to do good dressage but he's stiff on the left rein. You need to get him going forward properly and in a good outline to help build up his muscles.

Trainer: Joanna Jackson

A horse needs to be supple so that he can use his joints and muscles correctly. Any stiffness makes it difficult for him to move his body smoothly and energetically. It also makes it difficult for you to keep your balance, give the aids effectively and feel what the horse is doing underneath you.

If we don't exercise our bodies we start to feel stiff and it's just the same for horses. Muscles, bones and joints are living structures. They adapt to exercise and need to be trained for the job we want them to do.

It's very common for horses to be stiffer on one side than the other. With careful riding you can improve this, but if your horse hasn't done a lot of schooling it will take time to improve his flexibility and the tone of his muscles. This work has to be done slowly and carefully to avoid putting any strain on the horse's body.

Stiffness can also be a result of tension. Your horse could be tense because he's excited, worried or resisting your aids. To get the best out of him you have to learn to recognise when he's tense and teach him to relax and accept your aids.

Hannah Bond has owned seven-year-old Finn for six months. Before Hannah bought him, Finn had only been lightly hacked and schooled. Hannah would like to work on Finn's schooling to get him more established with a view to doing some dressage competitions.

In today's lesson Hannah and Joanna are going to work on exercises to encourage Finn to be more relaxed and supple. They also want to work on transitions, straightness and balance to generally improve Finn's way of going.

Private Lessons

Give your horse time in walk before the real work starts

The lesson

GETTING STARTED

Hannah works as a physiotherapist so she understands the importance of building up correct muscle tone. She is also very aware of the importance of warming up and working the muscles properly.

Finn's problem is that he's stiff on the left rein and tends to get more unbalanced on the right. To help him loosen up, Hannah usually starts off with plenty of time in walk. Joanna agrees this is a good idea. She tells Hannah that she should always take her time getting Finn warmed up and free from tension before she tries to work on anything else.

Joanna's tip

■ When you first get on your horse, allow five or ten minutes to walk him round on a loose rein. This gives his muscles a chance to warm up and become flexible before you start working them. If the weather is cold and your horse is clipped, you should always cover his back with a blanket or exercise sheet.

Leaning on the rein can be a sign that your horse is unbalanced

Here Finn is drifting to the outside on the circle

When Hannah keeps her outside rein she can stop him drifting out through turns

TROTTING ON

With Finn warmed up it's time to start the trot work. He is still building up muscle so he finds schooling hard work. Finn finds it quite difficult to work on a circle: he gets unbalanced and, to compensate, tries to support himself by leaning on the rein.

To prevent this, Joanna says to keep the circles large and avoid too much trotting on the circle at this stage in Finn's training. If Finn starts to lean on the rein

Hannah must give a half-halt and then relax the rein contact. Doing this will mean she's not hanging onto Finn's mouth, allowing the contact to become deadened. "Keep your elbows soft and think of your reins being like pieces of elastic," says Joanna.

Joanna sees Finn is drifting to the outside on circles and corners. She explains that this is because he's finding it

quite difficult to bend and use his body properly.

"When you're on a circle or corner don't let him drift," she tells Hannah. "Look at the line you want to take and, if he's drifting to the outside of that line, be ready for him. Keep him straight by putting your outside leg on and holding your outside rein out to the side to help you keep the contact."

SOFTLY SOFTLY

At the moment Finn finds it hard to work in a correct outline with his poll as the highest point. As it's difficult for him to stay soft in this outline, tension creeps in. Finn finds it much easier to work deep, with his head and neck held lower. Joanna explains that working like this will help to build up muscle where he needs it on his neck and back.

Joanna asks Hannah to give the reins forward and down towards the bit to gently encourage Finn to stretch. "His neck needs to feel boneless, like you could position it anywhere," she says. "You shouldn't feel any stiffness there." She explains that the reins are used to encourage the horse to stretch and loosen up. They are not used to pull the horse's head down.

Joanna reminds Hannah to praise Finn when he relaxes and becomes free and loose in his neck. "Praise him so he understands what you want and has the confidence to relax and let go," she explains.

Joanna's tip

You should be able to lighten your contact without your horse changing his outline

■ Remember that you and your horse are a partnership, so don't let yourself do all the work. If you feel your horse is setting in the neck and leaning on your hand you mustn't carry him. Using half-halts allows you to lighten your contact with your horse's mouth. It also activates the horse's hindlegs.

CANTER TRANSITIONS

Hannah says she has been having trouble with transitions into canter so Joanna asks her to try a few. The canter transitions are good and Joanna doesn't see any problem with them.

Joanna says this is because Finn is loosened up and his trot is active and powerful. If the trot is good the transition to canter will be good. The problems arise when the trot gets too speedy. The impulsion is lost and it causes Finn to carry more weight on his forehand. This makes it difficult for him to keep his balance, especially if he's asked to make a transition to canter.

It's important that Finn learns to carry more weight behind and not get onto his forehand. Hannah has to be quick to feel when he's leaning on her hands and must remember to sit up tall.

When the trot is good you'll find canter transitions get much easier

Private Lessons

DON'T LEAN ON ME

Joanna notices that Finn is putting more weight on Hannah's inside rein. This is the opposite of what he should be doing. "If he's leaning on the inside, go down the long side and do some counter bending," says Joanna. She reminds Hannah that she will need to keep her inside leg slightly back when she's doing this to stop the quarters from swinging in.

"When you come back to true bend he should be softer in your inside rein and you should have more weight in your outside rein," she explains.

Hannah is given another exercise when Finn starts leaning on the rein. "This time, if he gets heavy on the inside, try asking for even more bend to the inside," she says. "You're bending him into it to get him to stop leaning and encourage him to let go."

Counter bending is a good way to get your horse to take weight in the outside rein

Joanna adds that it's important Hannah still keeps the outside rein when she's doing this exercise. "No matter what, you must keep the rein that the horse doesn't want to take," she explains.

BALANCING ACT

It's important Hannah doesn't let Finn lean because this is when he gets unbalanced. When Finn is unbalanced he doesn't use his body properly and he drifts out through corners so he doesn't have to bend.

Joanna tells Hannah it's important she thinks of Finn's hindlegs following in the tracks of his forelegs. She explains that when he goes onto three tracks it's a sign that he's stiffening against Hannah's hand and leg aids. When this happens Hannah needs to open her outside rein slightly and keep her outside leg back to control Finn's quarters.

Here you can see Finn is on three tracks around the corner

Bending your horse towards his heavy rein can help make him lighter in your hand

Holding the rein slightly further out to the side gives Hannah more control

Riding to any kind of marker can test your accuracy

Another tip Joanna suggests is for Hannah to use the three-quarter line of the school, rather than always sticking to the outside track. This calls for more accurate riding, in order to keep the horse straight.

"If you are riding to a marker and you're not getting there, the horse is drifting. Try riding really accurately and use the markers to test yourself," says Joanna.

Joanna tells Hannah that when she is riding Finn she should imagine having a set of old-fashioned scales in her hands. "The weight in the scales needs to be 50/50 for them to be balanced," she says. "At the moment Finn is more like 70/30 because he's much stiffer on one side than the other."

Joanna says the ultimate aim is for Hannah to have slightly more weight in her outside rein, but for the moment Hannah must concentrate on getting a more equal feeling in her hands.

THE VERDICT

Finn's lack of suppleness is the main problem. Hannah will be able to improve this, but there is no way of cutting corners. It is going to take time. Joanna says that once Finn becomes more supple his whole way of going will improve.

Joanna thinks Hannah is doing very well with Finn. "Hannah being a physiotherapist definitely helps because she understands so much about muscles," Joanna adds.

Homework

Hannah usually lunges Finn twice a week and Joanna thinks this is good for him. In their schooling sessions Hannah needs to do plenty of exercises to help Finn to become more supple. Joanna says counter bending will be useful for this and Hannah can also introduce more circles and serpentines as Finn's muscles get stronger.

Although he's stiffer in one direction, Hannah should remember to work Finn equally on both reins. She must be careful to correct him when he starts to get heavy and unbalanced and reward him when he softens. Hannah needs to practise riding accurately and learn to be quicker to react with her outside leg and hand to stop Finn drifting.

Flying start

Problem: Your horse is bold cross country. However, he hurdles fences and you're unsure how to tackle bigger, more technical combinations and fences without coming unstuck

Trainer: Matt Ryan

Matt's tip

■ Think of each fence as part of a complex, even if it isn't. That way, you'll sit up on landing and concentrate on riding forward
■ The more accurate a line you need for a complex, the more momentum you should ask for.

There's an art to riding cross country safely and, once you get to the level of bigger, technical fences and combinations, there is a lot more to the sport than kicking on and hoping for the best. Each jump, whatever its size or complexity, must be treated with respect and approached thoughtfully.

When you're walking the course, consider not only the line or strides you're going to take, but the potential problems you may encounter. Is your horse likely to spook at a ditch between fences or is he wary of jumping into wooded areas? Think about all these likely scenarios and be ready to correct them as you ride the course. By planning ahead like this you will help prevent a disaster and stay in the saddle.

For Robyn McLean and King such forward planning is essential. Bold and cocky cross country, King naturally assumes he knows best and uses his racing background to hurdle fences. Robyn's job is to anticipate his mistakes and have a plan of action in place should things go wrong.

Robyn McLean and 16-year-old Thoroughbred gelding King make a confident double act. They both love cross country and compete in hunter trials up to 2'9". King was bred as a point-to-point horse and really throws himself at fences in true hurdler fashion.

Thanks to Mr and Mrs Bickham at Hilltop cross-country course, Ledbury, Herefordshire, for their help with this feature. For information, tel: 01531 632291 or visit www.hilltopxcledbury.co.uk

Robyn is keen to progress to bigger and more technical fences, but isn't sure how to go about this safely.

The lesson

FIRST THINGS FIRST

Before Robyn begins jumping, Matt explains what he wants to see in her position. Cross-country riding is all about safety, and Matt has developed a three-point plan to give riders the best possible chance of staying in place should the horse make a mistake:

■ Keep your legs forward, on the girth. Stick out your toes if you need to kick on instead of moving your legs back. Your legs are your 'seatbelt'

■ Hands must be soft so you can give with your reins, allowing the horse the freedom of movement to get himself out of trouble

■ Keep your upper body upright and imagine it is your shock absorber. Unfold the second you land over a fence and sit up, ready to control the horse for the next fence

THEY'RE OFF

Watching Robyn warm up, Matt is happy with her general riding position. Robyn never really leaves the saddle and that's great for security.

The first jump in the lesson is an innocent-looking log and rails combination and King really attacks it. Already it's clear that King's point-to-point roots have affected his cross-country style; he stands off from fences and launches himself at them. This may get King into trouble cross country and will affect his chances in the show jumping ring should the pair try eventing. Robyn should work on making him shorten his stride into fences.

It's obvious that impulsion isn't the problem here, and Matt praises Robyn's positive attitude. "Keep it aggressive but not wild," he says. "Cross country is all about calculated risks." Robyn needs to work on King's turns too, as he's a bit cheeky at the moment and his steering is prone to failure.

SPOOKY GOINGS ON

The next fence the pair have to tackle is a tyre jump, followed by a narrow rail fence and a sudden drop into a gully with a stream running through it. As with all cross-country jumps, Matt advises Robyn to stop and think before she jumps it to analyse what could go wrong. This way, Robyn will be able to devise a plan of action should King make a mistake and will be able to correct him quickly.

So what could go wrong here? Robyn predicts that King will be forward going over the tyres but may spook when he sees what's behind the rails. "With this kind of fence, always assume the horse is going to spook at what's behind – be it a drop or water – and leave a leg on the rails," says Matt. "You need to be sitting up so you don't pitch forward if the horse makes a mistake."

King jumps the combination cleanly but is a bit taken aback by the drop into the gully. However, because Robyn anticipates this, she manages to compensate for King's wariness by riding strongly with her legs.

"You're still taking off too early," says Matt. "Try to get King in closer to the jump by increasing momentum in the approach. You need to shorten him up so he gets in closer to the fence."

TAKE A DIVE

Robyn and King prepare for a bank fence (this bank is a step up, one stride on the top and a step down). While jumping up onto this bank, Matt advises Robyn that she should resist the temptation to lean forward as there's no time on the top of the bank to unfold. He also reminds her to lean back off the drop, keeping her upper body at a right angle to the ground.

It seems a lot to remember but, if your horse stumbles or makes a mistake at this kind of fence, you have a better chance of staying put if you sit up. It's important, too, to let the reins slide through your fingers on a drop down so you don't jab the horse in the mouth. If you need to take up the slack after a drop, draw your hands back rather than trying to gather up the reins, as this is less risky.

For a start, Robyn approaches the bank in trot and King makes it look easy. Again, Matt praises Robyn's position – she's giving with her hands and really leans back off the drop.

The only criticism Matt has of their performance is that King is very confident and

tends to take the initiative. He can get a little above himself and this may cause problems as the jumps get bigger and more technical. "You need to discipline a horse to listen to you," says Matt.

"You are the pilot and he needs to know that you are in charge."

Private Lessons

AT AN ANGLE

■ Next is a tricky combination which needs to be jumped at a sharp angle, and Robyn has her reservations. It's a step up followed by a big log fence which needs to be ridden aggressively. "Get up some pace and you'll find it easier to stay in a straight line," says Matt.
"Fences that need a lot of accuracy like this also need momentum, so really attack it."
Robyn's first attempt sees her jump up the bank (pic 1) then refuse at the logs (pic 2). Matt tells her to use her right rein and

point King at the fence. She tries it again, but he refuses four times in a row. Robyn is hesitant about the angle she's got to jump the logs (pic 3) and King senses this but, on the fifth time, Robyn cracks her nerves and they sail over it (pic 4).
"You were a bit too soft with him then," says Matt. "You've got to nip any resistance in the bud and teach the horse it won't be tolerated. Aim to be a good leader, not a dictator, and win the trust and respect of your horse by teaching him that he has to listen to you."

DITCHES

■ When training a horse to jump a ditch, Matt advises riders to approach it in walk first to let your horse have a look. King is used to ditches, but it's always worth letting the horse have a look and a sniff if you can. Once he has familiarised himself with the ditch, King pops over (pic 1).

If your horse isn't so bold, Matt advises you to praise him for every step forward and only tick him off if he goes backwards or sideways. Aim to build the horse's confidence and lead him to believe it was his idea to jump.

A confident King flies over two bigger ditches (pic 2 & 3). The problem Robyn has is that King can be too confident. She must keep him in check and not trust his judgement too much. She should also keep her reins soft so that if King jumps big she doesn't jab his mouth.

THE VERDICT

Matt has certainly given Robyn plenty to think about and work on during future cross-country sessions.

She and King both have the ability and confidence to compete successfully.

Robyn just needs to harness King's enthusiasm and work on channelling his energy so he gives each fence more thought and respect.

Homework

Robyn needs to work on getting King closer into fences before he takes off. she should also sit slightly more upright when coming up steps and ask for more impulsion and control.

As King has a tendency to be over-confident and take control of a situation, he needs to learn that Robyn is actually the one in charge and he must listen to her.

Calming influence

Problem: Your horse is the strong, sensitive type. He has bags of energy but it's not always easy to keep all that power under control.

Trainer: Joanna Jackson

All horses have different characters and temperaments. Some are naturally calm and lazy while others are highly–strung and buzzing with energy. Your horse's nature will dictate the way you ride him and being able to adapt to suit your horse is a major part of your skills as a rider. Sensitive horses can be a challenge. The rider has to be very quick to react but, at the same time, be tactful and careful with the aids. If the horse also has a tendency to be strong it makes the rider's job even harder.

If your horse is difficult to control there is no point in trying to fight strength with strength – you'll be fighting a losing battle. Some clever riding will get you the best results and win your horse's confidence.

Kate Proctor owns Paddy, a 16.3hh seven–year–old ID gelding. Kate has had Paddy for three years, although he has had nearly two years off work because of an injury. Kate and Paddy compete in riding club dressage, show jumping and working hunter classes.

Kate's ambition is to do some low-level affiliated show jumping.

The aim of today's lesson is to help Kate to get Paddy to slow down, soften and relax. He's a big horse and he is very sensitive but he needs to be more obedient to Kate's aids. Joanna would like to work on getting Paddy to be more responsive. This will help Kate with her flatwork and her jumping.

The lesson

GETTING SETTLED

As Kate and Paddy warm up in walk, trot and canter, it's clear that he's feeling full of himself. His paces are quite hurried and he looks like he would rather do his own thing than listen to what Kate is asking.

Kate says that Paddy can get uptight and strong. Joanna explains that it's easier for Paddy to go faster than move with controlled energy and impulsion. She wants Kate to work on keeping Paddy calm and going steadily. "Start by trying to slow down the tempo of his trot and canter," says Joanna. While Kate is working on this, Joanna reminds her to keep the correct bend. "Try to think of keeping Paddy bent around your inside leg," she tells her.

Joanna explains that speed causes Paddy to get long and flat in his outline.

"We need to think about maintaining the energy but, at the same time, work on getting him to slow down and relax," says Joanna.

To help Kate do this Joanna asks her to ride lots of transitions. This will get Paddy really listening to her. "Work on your halt transitions too," Joanna says. She explains that practising halt will help train Paddy to be more obedient and responsive to Kate's aids.

Horses can often use speed as an evasion

Joanna's tip

■ Impulsion is the powerful upward and forward thrust that comes from a horse's hindlegs. When your horse is going too fast, the impulsion decreases as his steps get quicker. Impulsion is important because it's the energy that gives your horse the ability to move and respond correctly to your aids. Riding plenty of transitions is a useful way to improve it.

Riding plenty of transitions, especially halt, when you're schooling is a useful way to keep your horse's attention and improve his way of going

READY FOR WORK

Paddy is starting to relax and listen so Joanna asks Kate to ride a 20m circle in trot. "As you pass over the centre line, give and retake the reins," she says. Joanna explains to Kate that Paddy shouldn't get faster when she does this. "Don't let him speed away with you when you soften the reins. Make sure you're ready to hold him with your seat and legs if you need to," she says (see panel, right).

The tempo of Paddy's trot is improving all the time. Joanna gives Kate a few more tips that will help her to maintain a better speed and rhythm. "As you're trotting round try not to tip forwards. Think of keeping your upper body tall and imagine you're rising up and back so you can use your weight to slow down the trot," she tells her. Joanna adds that if Kate can rise more slowly it will also help.

Joanna asks Kate to stay on the circle until she feels happy with the trot. "When you're ready go large, but don't let Paddy use it as an excuse to go faster," she tells her. "Think of keeping the same rhythm and if he gets strong, go back on a circle or ride a transition back to walk."

Joanna's tip

■ Giving and retaking the reins is a good way to test that your horse is carrying himself. Your aim is for the horse's head to stay in the same position when the rein contact is relaxed. This shows that he is not heavy and leaning on your hands. It will also show that you're not just holding his head in place.

To do it, give your hands forwards about 20cm towards the bit, hold them there for a couple of strides then return to normal. Your horse's head carriage should stay the same and his rhythm and speed should not alter. When you do this your seat and lower leg need to be in a good, secure position.

Before you give and retake both reins you can test whether your horse is ready by giving one rein at a time. Offering each rein like this will show whether your horse is in self-carriage.

Giving and retaking the reins is a useful exercise to check if your horse is carrying himself. Here Paddy lowers his head and is not in self-carriage

Sitting tall as you rise will help you to slow down your horse's trot

Private Lessons

THE POWER OF COMMUNICATION

When Paddy gets tense Joanna suggests that Kate should reassure him with a pat. Joanna comments that it seems to mean a lot to Paddy when Kate gives him just a small pat on the neck or talks to him.

Paddy is keeping a much better rhythm now and Joanna thinks it's time to give him a rest. "Letting him have a walk and a stretch is a reward for him now that he has relaxed," she says.

"Giving your horse some time to chill out during a schooling session is a good idea," says Joanna. "If you overwork your muscles they soon get sore and tense, and it's just the same for horses." Joanna believes that giving any horse lots of short breaks is always a good idea. "When you feel you've achieved something and your horse has worked well, a short break is good for relaxing his muscles. It's also a reward for your horse for his good work and will help make him more willing," she adds.

Joanna reminds Kate that, even though Paddy is having a rest, she must still make sure his walk stays active.

Reward your horse for good work with a rest and a pat

FEEL THE RHYTHM

Above: Kate has now got Paddy's full attention
Left: If your horse gets strong, use half-halts and then be soft with your reins

Joanna asks Kate to pick up canter again. Paddy immediately gets strong and Joanna warns Kate not to get into a pulling match with him. "If he's strong, take a half-halt and then be soft with your reins so he can't pull against you," she says (pic above).

Paddy responds to this and the canter is much better. "The canter looks much lighter now that he's carrying himself and he is really using his hindlegs," Joanna says.

Kate is keeping Paddy in a better rhythm now. Joanna says Kate can tell that there's a good rhythm when Paddy's breaths sound even and regular. Now Paddy is happy and relaxed, Kate can give and retake the reins and he will stay in balance and self-carriage (pic above right).

Joanna explains that some horses benefit from starting off in canter. Cantering often works well for getting a

horse to relax and settle in to a nice rhythm. This will vary from horse to horse and your instructor should be able to advise you on what works best for your horse.

Kate makes a transition to trot. Paddy's trot steps are now much bigger and more expressive than they were at the beginning of the lesson and, this time, the trot isn't getting any faster.

Joanna wants to test whether Kate can keep Paddy in this rhythm and tempo and asks her to ride a few lengthened strides. Joanna warns Kate that she will have to be very careful with her aids because Paddy is so sensitive and he can easily become tense.

Paddy is listening to Kate now and she is able to get him to lengthen and shorten when she wants him to (pic below). Joanna says there's no way he would have let her do this at the beginning of the lesson.

THE VERDICT

Joanna is pleased with Paddy's progress. Kate has done a good job of getting him to settle down and listen to her.

Paddy can get strong and fast, and it's important Kate doesn't get into a battle with him. If she can teach him to be softer by using more half-halts and transitions, she should be able to get him out of this habit.

Although he's a big horse, Paddy can be a bit nervy and a reassuring pat from Kate makes all the difference and helps her to boost his confidence.

Some lengthened strides prove Paddy's obedience

Homework

Kate needs to work on getting Paddy to be more obedient. Joanna wants her to practise riding lots of transitions to help with this. Kate also needs to be aware of Paddy's speed and rhythm.

Paddy has naturally got lots of energy and expression in his paces. If Kate can learn to contain this energy Joanna thinks they should do very well with their dressage and jumping.

Weakest link

Problem: Your young event horse has great scope in the dressage arena and is fantastic across country, but a patchy show jumping performance often ruins your chances of success.

Trainer: Mia Korenika

To succeed in eventing you and your horse need to be equally competent at all three disciplines. All too often a faulty cross-country round, or untidy dressage test, sees a rider's hopes plummet faster than his placing – a problem all too familiar to Leicestershire-based farrier, Glyn Trundle. His talented young horse D is typical of many – she gives the dressage test careful consideration, can't wait to go cross-country but doesn't have much time for the show jumping phase.

While D has the scope to show jump well, she tends to pay the fences little respect and can be lazy. Glyn needs to devise a plan of action to encourage her to concentrate and be more careful. He thinks gridwork might help but finds it baffling, so is hoping Mia will be able to explain a couple of exercises that he can practise at home.

Glyn Trundle has owned six-year-old ID x TB mare D for four months. Glyn describes the chestnut mare as quirky – D can be difficult to handle but, when she puts her mind to it, she shows great scope. Glyn and D have evented at Pre-novice level and Glyn hopes they will make Intermediate level by the end of next year.

While D is careful in the dressage and fantastic at cross-country, her show jumping performance is patchy. The weekend before this lesson she had eight poles down at a Pre-novice event, but on a good day she'll clear the lot. Glyn would like advice on how to make D's jumping more consistent and encourage her to concentrate.

The lesson

GENTLE WARM UP

As Glyn and D warm up on the flat, Mia explains what she looks out for at the start of each lesson. "I look at the rider's position, how effective his aids are and watch how the horse works on the flat. How responsive is she? What are her turns and transitions like and can she move in a straight line? I usually spend the first half of the lesson concentrating on the rider's position and the horse's way of going before doing any jumping.

"It's important not to make any demands on the horse as you work in," Mia tells Glyn. "Warm up in walk, trot and canter on both reins and use the time to work on your horse's rhythm and think about how you are sitting. Keep a light contact and don't ask too much."

Mia is happy with Glyn's position – he is nicely balanced in the saddle and his lower leg position is good. "Keep your stirrups short and make sure your knee is relaxed, your hips are open and your ankles are soft. This way, your joints act as a shock absorber," says Mia.

"Your legs should be either on or off, don't niggle with your heels. Squeeze and expect to get an answer. If you don't get one, repeat the aid. Think of your transitions as a light switch – press and go."

D is balanced in walk and trot, but goes better on the right rein than the left in canter.

D is nicely balanced in trot

Glyn lifts his legs away from the saddle to help develop a deep seat

SITTING DEEP

Warm up over, and still working on the flat, Mia introduces the first exercise of the day to make sure Glyn is sitting deep in the saddle and help to drum home the 'legs should be either on or off' message. In walk, Mia asks Glyn to lift his legs off the saddle for the duration of one stride, then put them back again (pic left). This encourages him to feel his seat bones. "While you're doing this exercise, think about your hand and body position," explains Mia. She then asks Glyn to repeat the exercise in trot and canter.

HALF HALTS

Working on a 20m circle in walk, trot and canter, Mia asks Glyn to practise half-halts. "I want to see a half-halt followed by a definite forward movement," says Mia (see panel, below, for the aids).

The first time Glyn tries a half-halt he does too much and D slows right down. "Grow tall through your body, relax your legs and aim to get the horse to anticipate a forward movement after the half-halt," Mia explains.

Glyn's second attempt is better, and by the third time both horse and rider are starting to get it right. This is something Glyn can work on at home.

Next is an exercise to work on Glyn's position and balance before he starts jumping. While trotting and cantering on a circle, Mia asks Glyn to sit for a few strides, then stand in the stirrups for a few strides. Then the flatwork session's over and it's time to try some jumps.

Standing in the stirrups for a few strides, then sitting for a few strides will help your balance

THE AIDS FOR HALF-HALT

The half-halt is a useful tool to engage the horse's hocks

● Grow tall through your spine
● Close your fingers on the rein to contain the horse's forward movement, so he becomes more collected
● Relax your legs
● The horse will briefly pause in his forward movement, becoming contained by the rein aids, before you apply your legs again to ask for forward movement

Glyn tries to place D at the fence, rather than letting her find her own rhythm

POLE POSITION

As D is still fairly green and her rhythm is patchy, Mia sets up a polework exercise to help remedy this. Mia puts a single pole on the ground and asks Glyn to work in a circle and canter over the pole. "Don't try to place the horse," says Mia. "Working on a circle means the horse is already engaging her quarters, your job is simply to keep a good rhythm going, and that's what this exercise is all about."

D is working well so Mia turns the poles into a cross-pole fence and asks Glyn to repeat the exercise. To emphasise the importance of rhythm, and to stop Glyn trying to place D at the fence, Mia stands in the centre of the school, level with the fence, and asks him to watch her as he goes over the jump and count how many fingers she's holding up. This takes Glyn's concentration away from the fence, prevents him from interfering with D's approach and allows her to find her own rhythm to the jump.

Mia's tips

■ When riding on a circle, use your inside leg to create the bend, tickle the inside rein and keep a steady contact on the outside rein

■ Lots of riders find it tricky to keep a stable contact on the outside rein, so Mia asks Glyn to plant his outside hand on the horse's neck, then he can forget about it

Looking away from the fence will help your horse's rhythm

LINE 'EM UP

Mia sets up a line of poles and asks Glyn to canter over them, paying attention to the corner before the poles. He needs to ride D into the apex of the corner, then let her straighten up and canter in a good rhythm over the poles. "Turning corners well is important in show jumping," says Mia. "So use your inside leg to your outside rein through the corner to create power and look in the direction you want to end up."

Glyn and D try this exercise on both reins and, although Glyn needs to ride out of the corner a bit more positively, they're doing well, so Mia ups the pressure. First she puts a cross-pole in the middle of the line of poles, which poses no problem for D. Then Mia adds an upright at the end –

D proves Glyn wrong and jumps the grid successfully

Cantering over poles is a good introduction to gridwork

and still D finds it easy. Mia raises the cross-pole and adds an upright at the start to form a proper gridwork exercise. Now there's a bounce to an upright, then two strides to a cross-pole and another two strides to an upright. "Keep D in a rhythm, make sure the engine's running, but let the horse do the work," says Mia.

"Don't try to see a stride – let the horse jump in a rhythm and, if she makes a mistake, don't worry about it."

D goes all out to prove Glyn wrong and show everyone that she can jump like a stag. She is largely foot perfect over the grid until Mia raises both the cross-pole and the final fence. D knocks down the cross-pole and demolishes the final fence, then goes on to clip the cross-pole again but clears the final upright on her second attempt. Mia's pleased with this as D tried

really hard to clear both fences and was unlucky with the cross-pole. She drops the second and third fences down again and asks Glyn to jump the grid a couple more times to give D a confidence boost.

"My only criticism would be that D needs to come more from behind," says Mia. "When the engine's running you get a better, more rhythmic canter, but this comes with practice.

"In show jumping you need to find the technique that works for you. Ideally you want to keep the horse in a rhythm so she can jump from this, but it takes a lot of self-confidence not to try to place the horse at each fence. Think about your riding as you warm up before a class and don't worry if she hits a fence in the collecting ring as this may make her more careful in the arena."

THE VERDICT

Glyn is pleased with D's progress and feels they've both learned a lot from the lesson. Gridwork will no longer be such a baffling exercise and Mia's given him plenty of ideas he can take home. Gridwork certainly seems to make D concentrate more on her jumping and Glyn's lucky that he's got the confidence and secure seat needed to let her jump from a rhythm. D's proved that she does have the necessary scope to show jump well and, if Glyn can get her jumping consistently, they should have no problem reaching the next level in eventing.

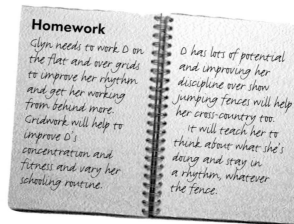

Homework

Glyn needs to work D on the flat and over grids to improve her rhythm and get her working from behind more. Gridwork will help to improve D's concentration and fitness and vary her schooling routine.

D has lots of potential and improving her discipline over show jumping fences will help her cross-country too.
It will teach her to think about what she's doing and stay in a rhythm, whatever the fence.

Back to school

Problem: You want your horse to be more obedient to your aids and to have more consistent rhythm and bend – but he isn't making it easy for you.

Trainer: Angela Niemeyer

The way your horse moves, his conformation and his level of training all affect the way you ride him. But who's making the decisions? All too often it's the horse, not the rider, who is calling the shots.

Your horse can easily influence your position and riding without you even noticing. The key to being a better rider is learning to be aware of what's going on underneath you and knowing how to react to get the best out of your horse.

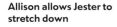
Allison allows Jester to stretch down

The lesson

WARMING UP

Angela asks Allison to warm up as she would normally do at home. She's pleased to see that Allison usually spends five or 10 minutes in walk, letting Jester loosen up and relax on a long rein. "Now he's got used to his new surroundings you can hold the reins at the buckle," says Angela. Jester really starts to stretch down (pic left).

As they walk round, Angela reminds Allison to remember to use her seat. "Push him a little more from your seat, take it forwards as if you were zipping up your trousers and squeeze with your legs. Think of it as if you're opening up a channel with your seat and you're pushing the horse through it with your legs."

Allison can feel the difference now, she's moving her hips more and going with Jester's movement. Angela explains that this allows the horse more freedom to move. "This is more like the type of walk the judge would be looking for," Angela tells her. "It's really moving on at a good marching pace."

When Allison's hips are relaxed, her legs lie against Jester's side

Allison Lowther owns Jester, a 16.2hh, eight-year-old Irish x TB gelding. Jester hasn't done a lot of schooling and this is the first time Allison has owned a young horse. They enjoy eventing and riding club competitions and have been placed in unaffiliated dressage.

Allison would like to do more dressage. Jester has nice paces and Allison feels that, with some help, they could do much better. Allison describes Jester as quite stiff on the right rein and she has trouble getting him to bend right. Angela says this is a very common problem. In today's lesson she wants to show Allison some exercises she can do to help improve her position, control and the effectiveness of her riding.

MOVING INTO POSITION

Angela starts by asking Allison to ride some large serpentine loops. "I want you to practise turning him using only your weight and legs, not the reins," says Angela. She explains that, to turn left, Allison will need to put more weight on her left seatbone and use her right leg. "Remember it's your outside leg that moves the horse," she tells her.

Angela says she would like Allison to ride with longer stirrups, as her current short length is unbalancing her. But Allison finds she loses her stirrups if she rides any longer. Angela isn't surprised by this, she has noticed that Allison is quite tight in her hips. She explains that this tightness makes the rider sit on the horse rather like a clothes-peg, making the lower legs stick out like an upsidedown V. When the rider's hips are relaxed, the legs can more easily lie against the horse's sides, more like an upsidedown U.

Angela explains that Allison will be able to ride Jester forward more effectively if she relaxes her hips. "If you clench your bottom and push stiffly, you cannot drive the horse," she explains. "The aim is to take the horse forward with your hips, you have to be supple and strong in your body to do that," she adds. "Imagine you're sitting on a tube of toothpaste and you want to squeeze some out. You need to wrap your legs around the horse and bring your lower leg inwards."

Angela suggests that riding without stirrups at home will help Allison's position, as would some lunge lessons. This would help her legs to swing and lie more closely around Jester's sides. Achieving flexibility is hard work but it's worth it in the long run and would reduce the effort Allison has to put into her riding.

Riding serpentines helps with control

Private Lessons

Angela shows Allison how to lift her thighs in front of her

Lifting legs alternately will deepen the seat

Angela's tip

■ According to Angela, most horses are left handed, meaning they have a natural crookedness which makes them hold their bodies like an S. It means the horse will usually find it easier to bend to the left and will be stiffer to the right. You can improve this by making sure you don't have too much inside bend when you're on the left rein and encouraging the horse to accept your outside (right) rein.

TIME FOR EXERCISE

As Jester will stand safely, Angela decides to give Allison some exercises to do.

"Rest your hands behind you on the cantle and bring both of your thighs up in front of you. Hold them slightly out to the side then lower them down again." (Pic above left.) Allison finds this difficult and Angela explains it's because she's lacking strength in the lower back. Doing this exercise will help her to strengthen this area. Allison should aim to build up her strength gradually until she can stay upright without holding the saddle while she brings her legs up and holds them in that position.

Angela has another good exercise to improve the suppleness of Allison's hips. "Take your feet out of the stirrups and lift one leg over the horse's withers," she says (pic above right). "Do this alternately, keeping hold of the pommel with your opposite hand. Practising moving opposite hands and legs together will help your coordination. Try to bring your leg up straight, then bend it over the horse's neck. Start slowly then, as you get looser, try doing it more quickly. The aim of the exercise is to widen the base of your seat in the saddle and stretch your legs."

TROTTING ON

Allison rides forward into trot and Angela reminds her to sit tall in the transition. Angela now wants to help Allison get Jester into a more rounded outline. She can see that Allison is driving him forward but, because her rein contact is quite loose, she's letting a lot of the energy escape. To contain this energy, Angela

asks Allison to shorten her reins and resist a little more so Jester has to give and becomes rounder in his outline.

If Allison can be more aware of her position, it will help. "Sit with your chest forward and keep a firm but elastic outside contact. Don't be rigid in your arm and shoulder, make it comfortable for the horse," she says.

Allison tries the transition again. This time Jester is much rounder. "He seemed more willing to be round without me asking as much," she says.

STRAIGHTENING UP

Allison rides a large circle on the left rein and Angela sees that she's holding her inside leg back. She also notices Allison is slightly collapsing on the left and is hanging her body over to the right. She explains that this is a common fault. "It happens because of the horse's natural crookedness," she says. "Most horses naturally push the rider to the right. When you're used to riding without help on the ground, it becomes difficult to know whether you're sitting straight."

When Angela checks, she sees that Allison's right stirrup is longer than the left. This is because Jester is pushing her over to the right. Angela shortens the stirrup and asks Allison to sit to the left. Allison is now sitting straight but, because she has got so used to sitting to the right, she feels as if she's too far to the left.

Angela says that Allison will need to practise sitting to the left and stepping into her left stirrup until Jester is unable to move her and she gets used to the feeling of sitting straight.

Angela points out that Allison collapses on one side, and straightens her up

SQUARING UP

Angela has another exercise to test Allison's control. She asks her to ride a large square, halting at each corner then turning and riding a straight line to the next corner. Jester tries to turn before Allison gives him the command and Angela reminds her to be sure he doesn't do anything until he's asked.

Angela shows Allison that if she keeps her elbows bent, and holds them closer to her body, it will give her more stability and make it harder for Jester to take control of the proceedings. Angela shows Allison what a difference this makes by pulling on the reins as if she was a strong horse. Angela's first pull tips Allison forward out of the saddle.

"Now anchor yourself by bending your elbows and pushing your stomach forward," she says. Now Angela tries again and, this time, she can't shift Allison's position, even by leaning all her weight against her. Angela explains that, other than your legs, your stomach is the strongest part of your body you have to ride with. "It's not your back that holds your posture, it's your stomach – that's what you need for stability so you can ride a horse into the contact."

Allison practises riding the square exercise again to get Jester listening to her aids. Angela reminds her to concentrate on keeping Jester straight. The halts are getting better now and Allison is sitting straight and upright. Now that Allison is more in control, and Jester is obeying her, Angela asks her to try riding the squares without the halts in walk and then, as her accuracy improves, in trot.

GETTING INTO THE RHYTHM

Allison circles right in rising trot. She gives with the right rein to encourage Jester to take it forward. He is losing the rhythm and starts to run a little, so Allison needs to use her outside rein to slow him down. She resists with her seat and leg for the second she sits, at the same time closing her hands around the reins to give a half-halt.

To get Jester really bending around Allison's right leg, Angela reminds her to push her right leg against his body and use more right rein. Angela says Jester will find this easier as he becomes more

supple laterally. She tells Allison to spiral him inwards on the circle and then spiral out again – this will really help him bend.

Jester's trot is getting more relaxed now and Allison is finding it easier to position him and keep him in a steady rhythm. Angela asks her to ride forward into walk. She explains to Allison that she should think of driving him downward into a shorter frame so he takes more weight on his hindlegs. "This means the horse is able to carry himself, so when you allow the reins and ask for walk he will be prepared," she says. Jester isn't used to being driven forward and, at first, he tries to hollow in the transition. Angela explains how the transition should feel: "The rider sits and drives into the rein so the contact feels stronger, the neck and reins fill out and the horse feels almost bunched up, then you allow him to walk. You stop moving with your hips and allow with your reins."

Jester is accepting the contact much more now and, to finish off, Angela asks Allison to get him to take the rein even further down before allowing him to relax on a loose contact.

When Allison is not anchored in her seat, Angela can pull her forward out of the saddle. With her stomach pushed forward, and her elbows bent, Allison is much more secure

Jester's trot relaxes as his rhythm improves

THE VERDICT

Angela says Allison has done a good job today. "There is a lot for her to take on board and she has coped very well. Jester hasn't really learned to be in a contact, so Allison will need to teach him to come more into the rein so he can become more connected. She achieved this towards the end of the lesson and Jester started to move with more swing. I needed to show Allison how to get Jester to be more obedient to her aids and I'm very happy with the result."

Allison is also pleased with their progress. "By the end of the lesson I could feel Jester's belly against my legs, he seemed much more rounded and more responsive to my aids."

Angela's tip
■ We all get into the habit of looking down the horse's neck and at our hands. To develop your feel, practise working on your awareness of where your body is and what it is doing, without relying on your eyes

Life in the fast lane

Problem: Your horse is strong, forward–going and loves approaching fences at full pelt, but this is having a negative effect on your confidence.

Trainer: Mia Korenika

Mia asks Katie to soften her elbows and hands

A bold, forward–going horse is an asset for show jumping, but there's a fine line between feeling in charge and out of control if your horse is the type to see a fence and go. It seems a shame to thwart the horse's enthusiasm – after all, he is only doing his job – but such exuberance can mean a white-knuckle ride for the jockey.

It may be tempting to cling on, hope for the best and let the horse make all the decisions, but that's when accidents happen and poles fall. Instead, you need to find a rhythm, ride the horse into each fence and go with him, instead of fighting all the way.

Milly is blessed with heaps of scope and enthusiasm, but Katie feels like a nervous motorbike pillion passenger – not in control and going too fast.

Katie is hoping that Mia will be able to give her advice on controlling Milly, especially on the approach to a fence, to make their show jumping less rushed and give Milly every chance to find the right stride and round her back over a fence. This will help Katie's confidence and make jumping fun again.

Katie O'Brien has owned seven-year-old Irish Sport Horse, Milly, for 18 months. The pair compete in unaffiliated novice dressage and BSJA show jumping classes. As Katie has recently had a baby and Milly has been out of action due to an abscess on her hock, the pair haven't had much time together to form a relationship.

A typical Irish Sport Horse, Milly is confident, forward-going and loves jumping. However, she tends to come into jumps too fast and take out strides. As Milly is strong, this is beginning to erode Katie's confidence. She needs to feel more in control, rather than like a high-speed passenger.

The lesson

FIRST THINGS FIRST

As Mia watches Katie warm up she explains that they will spend the first part of the lesson concentrating on flatwork. This way, Katie can think about her position and Milly's way of going before they even try a fence. Katie needs to work on collecting Milly and controlling her speed so, once they have worked in, Mia introduces an exercise to encourage Milly to collect and soften.

"In trot, close your fingers around the outside rein and lift your hand slightly," explains Mia. "Sit deep and use your hands and seat to ask the horse to collect for a couple of strides, then allow the horse to go forwards and soft for a few strides."

Mia asks Katie to repeat this exercise a few times before they try it in canter. "If you find it difficult to keep a steady contact on the outside rein, plant your outside hand on Milly's neck so you can maintain the contact," she suggests.

Mia also concentrates on Katie's position. Katie is a tidy rider and has a secure leg position but, because Milly is strong, she has a tendency to round her shoulders and fix her elbows. She needs to sit tall and try to soften her elbows and hands.

TAKE A BRAKE

Mia's next exercise is designed to break the vicious circle which is hampering Katie's jumping. What often happens is that Milly tanks into a fence, Katie pulls on the reins to say 'whoa' just before the jump and Milly mistakes this for a cue to jump. She takes off too early and misses a stride, often nearly unseating Katie in the process. This does nothing for Katie's confidence, so she's even more cautious on the next approach and Milly gets her stride wrong again.

Mia positions a small upright so that Katie can approach, in canter, on a circle. This is a great exercise for speedy horses. Working on a circle means the horse has to stay in a rhythm over the fence as there's no chance of a high-speed approach. It's a good way of slowing him down and getting him to think about what he is doing.

Mia asks Katie to pop over the fence from a 20m circle at A, canter the long side of the school, then ride another 20m circle (without a jump) at the other end of the school. Then she repeats the exercise, all the time asking Milly to collect for a few strides, then go forwards again.

Below: Katie approaches the jump, in canter, on a circle

Milly pops over the fence calmly

Private Lessons

TIME FOR GRIDWORK

Next up is a gridwork session to help slow Milly and teach her to consider her speed and stride. This grid consists of a pole, a bounce stride to an upright, followed by two more uprights. "I want to see you maintain a rhythm and sit with the horse," says Mia.

At their first attempt, Katie and Milly approach the grid in canter. Milly jumps the first fence then sets her jaw, resists the rein contact and runs out (pic A). They try again and this time jump it clear, albeit a bit too fast (pic B). Mia tells Katie to keep repeating the collect and soften exercise as she rides round the arena to steady Milly.

At the third attempt, Milly runs out before the final upright and Katie's confidence is disappearing fast. "Work Milly on a circle, in canter, ask her to collect – and try to relax," says Mia. When they try the grid for a fourth time, the same thing happens, so Mia asks Katie to circle away and use more inside leg. "On the circle, use your inside leg to create the bend, tickle the inside rein and keep a steady contact on the outside rein to keep Milly collected," says Mia. However, by now Katie's nerves are starting to fray and Milly can sense this. Katie needs to get a grip, think positive and be firm, but this isn't as easy as it sounds. "Even though Milly is fast, you need to use your legs to ride her round corners and into each fence," says Mia. "She's ducking out because you are sitting behind her movement, not moving with her."

Mia removes the pole on the final upright so Katie only has to ride through the jump wings. Millie canters through the grid, but is still on the speedy side. When they try again, Milly sets her jaw and runs out once more. Mia asks Katie to approach in trot. Katie is more confident and they clear the grid. Mia puts the final upright back up and, still in trot, they jump it clear (pic C).

Milly jumps the first part of the grid, then sets her jaw and runs out

Milly jumps the grid clear on their second attempt, but the pace is still too fast

Katie approaches the grid in trot and manages to kick on, close her eyes and make it over the last fence

Katie needs to use her legs on the approach to a fence

IT'S A FINE LINE

"As Milly goes like a bullet along a straight line of fences, it's difficult to convince Katie that she has got to keep the horse working, rather than sitting there thinking that she's going to bolt," explains Mia. "If you tell your horse 'no' all the time, she will simply fight against you.

"It is important to use your legs, even on a horse as forward-going as Milly. When riding on a circle you have to use your inside leg to get the bend, and this is why jumping on a circle is a good exercise for Katie, to remind her to use her legs before a fence."

MORE CIRCLE WORK

Katie and Milly go back to jumping on a circle as Mia sets up a parallel and asks Katie to approach on the left rein in canter. Despite a slightly patchy rhythm, it's a good approach.

"Use your inside leg to create impulsion and maintain the rhythm," says Mia. Next, Katie jumps an upright, circling towards it in canter and jumping it well. It's clear that Katie is more confident jumping on a circle than she is with gridwork, as Milly can't take a hold and just go. They try the fence a couple more times to finish on a high. Milly clips it once but Katie kicks on and they fly over.

Jumping on a circle boosts Katie's confidence and improves Milly's approach

THE VERDICT

Katie's confidence took a knock during the gridwork exercise but she's feeling more confident by the end of the lesson. Even though Katie has owned Milly for 18 months, they've both been out of action for a large chunk of that time, so haven't had long to get to know each other. Mia has given Katie lots of ideas to take away and try and Katie will be having regular lessons to build her confidence and rapport with Milly.

Homework

Katie should repeat the jumping on a circle exercise with lots of different fences, thinking about using her legs and trying to maintain a rhythm. She can gradually incorporate gridwork exercises into her schooling routine too – jumping from trot until she feels confident enough to canter. If Katie can crack her confidence, ride Milly into jumps and go with her, rather than fighting, they will be a successful pair.

Katie rides in a Market Harborough as she had problems developing her feel for a contact with Milly and they tended to set themselves against each other. The Market Harborough makes sure that Katie's rein aids are softer and helps to stop a fight between them.

Problem: Your horse has bags of ability but is young and inexperienced. The training you do now is important if she's to reach her maximum potential.

Trainer: Chris McGrann

Bright young thing

Good basic training is vital. Whatever you intend to do with your horse, be it jumping, dressage or simply hacking – training is just as important.

A horse may be born bursting with natural talent, paces to die for and the ability to jump to the moon, but on its own that isn't enough. As soon as a rider sits on his back, he is put off balance and he has to learn how to move well all over again.

In training a ridden horse we're showing him the best way to rebalance and carry himself and his rider. We're teaching him how to perform to the best of his ability, moving with lightness and ease, without restriction and tension. If the training we do is correct it will enhance the horse's paces, it should never restrict or spoil the way he moves.

Use the warm up to get your horse to relax, stretch and go forward

Harriet Burrows has owned her five-year-old TB mare, Dottie, since February. Harriet is an experienced rider and aims to compete successfully at affiliated eventing. Harriet bought Dottie as a potential event horse and they have already completed four Pre-Novice events, as well as doing some unaffiliated dressage and hunter trials.

Dottie has good paces, rhythm and activity but her head carriage varies and she can be heavy in Harriet's hand. Chris hopes to get her to be more confident and steady in the contact. He wants to encourage Dottie to find her own balance and help Harriet get the best from her.

The lesson

GETTING STARTED

As Harriet warms up in walk, Chris reminds her to give Dottie a chance to stretch and loosen her top line. Harriet is keen to get down to work with Dottie but Chris wants her to take her time and asks her to ride on a long rein. Chris explains that during the warm up phase Harriet's priority should be to keep the horse going forwards and to get her to relax and stretch while warming her muscles and loosening her joints. She also needs to be sure that Dottie is listening to her leg aids.

Dottie naturally tends to hold her head quite high. Chris comments that it can be tempting for the rider to shorten the reins to stop them looking around. Chris warns Harriet to be careful about shortening the reins at this stage, as it will just restrict Dottie's steps and make her tense.

Chris wants to see Dottie walking freely and actively forwards. He tells Harriet not to worry if she breaks into trot. "It doesn't matter, just go with her then return to walk," he says. Now that Dottie has had time to warm up on a loose rein Chris sees that she's getting more settled. "She's starting to loosen up and search down for the contact," he says.

Standing up in the stirrups is a good way to improve your balance and lower leg position. Take care you're not supporting yourself with the reins

BALANCING ACT

Dottie is getting more relaxed and ready to work so Chris asks Harriet to go forward into trot. He notices that Dottie isn't really listening to Harriet's leg aids. Chris explains

Dottie is beginning to relax and look for the contact

Private Lessons

that this is affecting Harriet's position. "When the horse isn't listening to you, your leg draws up in your attempt to get more of a response. But this actually makes it weaker," he says.

To help Harriet really establish her lower leg position and find her balance Chris suggests an exercise. "Try standing in the stirrups in trot," he says. "If you're in balance you can do it all day, but when your leg is up you can't do it." After a wobbly start Harriet soon stands up without a problem.

Dottie's trot is improving all the time and her movement is becoming more supple and afree. Chris says the reason she wasn't going forward at the beginning was because she was tense. "She came in with a high head carriage but now she's relaxed, listening to the legs and taking the rein contact," he says. "Her trot is really starting to get springy now," he adds.

Chris says it's important for Harriet to concentrate on riding Dottie forward so she doesn't end up just focusing on her head carriage. "You can check if she's on the aids by riding transitions," he says.

RIDER THINKING

Dottie is young and doesn't always concentrate. Chris says this is where Harriet's experience is a real advantage. "It's important the rider can feel what the horse is doing and how the horse reacts, so she can take appropriate action," says Chris.

As she's working, Harriet notices that Dottie isn't really paying attention. Her response is to ride forward onto a smaller circle. Chris explains that this is a good idea. "Just moving onto a small circle means Dottie has to concentrate. She has a very active brain and can easily be distracted. By asking her to do simple tasks that she understands Harriet can get her to concentrate," says Chris. "This also helps to bring about submission without the rider having to be strong and dominant," he adds.

To keep Dottie's attention Harriet uses the whole of the school. She rides lots of transitions and uses movements such as leg-yielding to really get her thinking.

Harriet uses the whole of the school to keep Dottie's attention

Moving onto a small circle gives Dottie something to think about

TESTING TIME

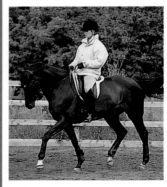

As the engagement, balance and activity of the trot improves, the pace starts to get more spring

Chris asks Harriet to ride Dottie on smaller circles. "Riding 10 or 12m circles will test the quality of the trot," he says. Chris keeps Harriet in rising trot so she has to use legs, rather than seat, to maintain the suppleness in Dottie's back.

Chris explains that 10m circles will show whether Dottie is able to maintain the rhythm, balance and engagement of the trot in preparation for doing some shoulder-in. "If the horse isn't capable of a 10m circle, shoulder-in will make her stiff because she hasn't got the ingredients to do it," he says. "Small circles are a good test because if you don't have enough engagement you can't do them. Also, you're not able to do them if the rhythm of your working trot is too fast."

Chris is pleased with the trot work. "Dottie is getting more lift now, the rhythm is super and the trot has a lovely spring," he says. But he warns Harriet not to be afraid to insist quietly if Dottie does not listen to a polite aid. "You have to give the horse a positive yes or no. If the rider is prepared to accept something that's just OK, the horse will accept that too."

Chris's tips
- Practise standing in your stirrups at any safe time – try it when you're out on hacks. Doing this will help improve your balance and leg position and will make your lower leg more secure. Resting on the hands is not allowed.
- Chris says it's a common fault to ride with your stirrups too long. This makes you less secure in the saddle and means it's more difficult for you to ride effectively

CANTER WORK

"Thoroughbreds like Dottie have been bred to gallop," says Chris. "To compete in other disciplines, we have to train them to take more of their weight onto their hindquarters and to collect." He comments that her rhythm in canter is good, but she's supporting herself by leaning on the reins, taking a heavy contact. Half-halts will encourage her to be lighter.

Chris asks Harriet to ride some shallow counter canter loops in from the track along the long sides of the arena. This exercise is good for encouraging Dottie to start to collect. Performing counter canter takes balance and suppleness. As Dottie starts to trust that she can balance herself without leaning on the contact, Harriet rewards her, confirming that's what she wants her to do. Dottie is looking a lot more supple and loose.

Chris explains that today's lesson is very quietly putting pressure on Dottie to get her attention on the aids. "If we tried to do too much too quickly with her she'd just become tense," he says. Chris tells Harriet not to be afraid to do half-halts and to use a lot more transitions. "Try doing a set number of trot steps, then walk, then do the same in canter and trot. This will test that you're really in control," he says.

Counter canter loops are a good test of balance

Dottie's rhythm is good but she supports herself by leaning on the reins

Chris's tips

■ Engagement is difficult to define. But basically it means that the horse isn't relying on his forelegs to pull him along – he's in correct balance and is using his hindlegs to push forward and create the power needed to perform his work.

Without engagement the horse carries his weight on the forehand making it difficult for him to maintain balance, rhythm, straightness and power necessary for the movements we ask.

Homework

Chris says it's important for riders to be aware of exactly what their horses are doing and why.

He says Harriet should continue to do more of the same work, concentrating on building up Dottie's suppleness and engagement. "Harriet needs to have confidence in what she's doing and check that Dottie is listening to her," says Chris. "she must be careful not to grip up with her leg," he adds.

Working on the rhythm of the paces using different sized circles and counter canter loops will be useful exercises. "You need a good quality canter to do this," says Chris. "if it starts to feel more difficult you know the canter isn't good enough."

THE VERDICT

Harriet is very pleased with Dottie. "She went nicely today and was a lot calmer and more relaxed than she can be. Her attitude was good too, she was obedient and responsive," adds a happy Harriet.

Chris thinks Dottie is coming on well and says that Harriet has established a good base to her training. He is also pleased with the improvement in the horse's level of confidence. "Because of the understanding and trust that's building up, Dottie is more willing to try the things she finds physically difficult. She has no problem lengthening and galloping, it's the collection we need to gradually work on as she gets stronger."

Doing the ground work

Problem: You want to learn how to get the best out of your horse and improve your performance at competitions.

Trainer: Chris McGrann

You may have been rushing around all day while your horse has been quietly eating and relaxing. Take a little time to get on the same wavelength

Carl Burrows has been riding for about five years and bought 12-year-old Briar three years ago. Briar is a 16.2hh ID x TB mare. The pair compete in unaffiliated events and Carl's aim is to do some affiliated Pre-novice events.

Today's lesson is aimed at helping Carl to ride more effectively at competitions. Chris wants to work on transitions to improve the natural rhythm and balance of both horse and rider. He also wants to help Carl to get Briar more obedient to his aids.

The work you put in at home is important preparation for competing. Having regular lessons from a good instructor is valuable for helping you and your horse get in tune. An instructor's expert eye can make a big difference to your performance – but what happens when the lesson is over? It's easier to get the best from your horse when someone on the ground is telling you what to do, but once you enter that competition arena you're on your own.

As riders it's important we understand what our horse is doing, what we are doing, why we're doing it and how it affects the horse. A good instructor doesn't just bellow instructions at you, he explains exactly what's happening with you and your horse and teaches you to think for yourself.

If you're not sure what you should be doing, flatwork can be a struggle. Often you hear people say that dressage is boring – in fact, it's only boring if you're not thinking about what you're doing and what you are trying to achieve. When you have identified your goals, flatwork can be a great challenge which has positive effects on your jumping as well as your dressage.

The lesson

THE WARM UP

Chris asks Carl to start off in walk to give horse and rider the chance to loosen up. Chris comments that many riders are tempted to skip the warm-up phase and get straight down to schooling. But this is not a good idea. "Walking for the first 15–20 minutes is not time wasted," says Chris. "It's an important time for the rider to think about their position and to assess how the horse is feeling today. Busy professional people like Carl may have had a hectic day at work but the horse has had a quiet day – they both need time to get into the same frame of mind."

Chris finds that a lot of people can ride well while their instructor is training them but when left to their own devices it all goes wrong. He believes it's important for riders to be taught how to think for themselves.

Chris makes his own assessment and asks Carl how he feels Briar is going. He wants Carl to think about Briar's reactions to his leg and rein aids. Is she relaxed? Is she giving him the same feeling in both reins? "When Carl rides without me here he has to be aware of what he's doing. There's no point in me telling him what to do all the time, he has to learn to think for himself," he explains.

Riding trot-to-halt transitions will activate your horse's body and his mind

Chris's tip

■ If you struggle to instinctively stay in a constant rhythm, try riding to music. The beat makes rhythm easier to judge. To check if you're keeping a good rhythm, get someone to video you riding. It's often easier to see changes in rhythm and speed than it is to feel them

READY FOR A TEST

Working on accuracy, rhythm and balance will improve Carl's test riding. Like most people, Carl works on schooling then thinks he has to do something different when he rides a dressage test. Chris explains this is not the case. "To me, a dressage test is basically walk, trot and canter," he says. "If you can do this correctly, working forward in an obedient, rounded outline then you're doing a test. So many people ride nicely at home, but as soon as they think of a test they freeze. If you can train your horse and yourself to use the arena properly and ride accurate movements all the time, there's no extra pressure when you do a test."

Chris asks Carl to ride lots of transitions. This will encourage Briar to use her body and her mind. He warns that, to begin with, the transitions shouldn't be too sharp. "Start by going from trot, to walk, to halt. When this is going well you can build it up to some trot-to-halt transitions, just as you would do in a test."

Chris is pleased with the way Carl is working. He is being positive and is rewarding Briar with a pat when he gets a good response. Chris also likes the freedom and rhythm that Carl is getting from Briar.

USING THE SCHOOL

The warm up over, Chris asks Carl and Briar to trot. He wants to see Carl really using the arena, riding straight lines and accurate corners. He asks Carl to concentrate on riding Briar forward into a good rhythm and reminds him to be aware of his own rhythm too. "Before you can dictate rhythm and balance to the horse, you have to be aware of your own rhythm and balance," he adds.

As they set off Carl is concentrating hard and Chris reminds him to breathe.

"It's really common for people to hold their breath when they ride," says Chris. "You often see riders red in the face and near to collapse when they come out of the show jumping arena."

Right: You should be aiming to keep a steady rhythm in all paces

Chris's tip

■ Working on riding better transitions will help everything you do. "If you can't do a polite transition when you're in the school, how can you expect to do one on a cross–country course?" asks Chris

Below: It's important to take time out in your lessons for a rest and for discussion

Private Lessons

MOVING ON

Chris gives Carl and Briar a breather and takes this opportunity to ask Carl what he's thinking. "Briar is going nicely forward. At times she's resisting my hands but so far, so good," replies Carl. Chris agrees, he thinks Briar's movement is free and forward, she just needs to be a little more consistent. He tells Carl he can achieve this by riding more transitions and more of the movements from his dressage tests, such as circles and changes of rein.

Chris asks Carl to ride some walk-to-halt transitions, and reminds Carl to prepare himself properly. "Your halt needs to be straight," says Chris. "Shorten your reins slightly so Briar's hindlegs are more engaged." He also warns Carl not to hurry the transition. "Take your time, half close your eyes so you can feel what's happening, then ask for halt. Imagine you're galloping and you want to get her back so you can jump a bounce fence – that's the feeling you're looking for."

Carl rides some good halt transitions and Chris asks him to try the same exercise in trot. Briar can sometimes get a little free and fast, so Chris warns Carl that he'll have to use lots of small half-halts. "Don't let the trot get any faster and remember to keep the rhythm."

THE NEXT STEP

Chris points out that Briar's stride length has increased since the start of the lesson. He explains this is because she's more in balance. "Now that she's propelling herself from behind her stride is longer. Having a good length of stride is important," he adds. "It's more comfortable for the rider than short choppy steps and it's also better for the horse. It means she uses less strides, so doing a cross-country course will be less tiring."

Chris wants Carl to work on riding straight lines ready for entering the dressage arena. "Use the fence as a guideline and look straight ahead," he says. "Then ride through the corner. Think of it like you'd corner in a car – if you've got the energy coming out of the turn you'll come out straight, if you haven't got enough power you'll lose your steering, so keep a constant leg contact."

When Carl has practised this a few times Chris asks him to bring the line in away from the track. "It has to be as straight as it was by the fence," he says.

Take the time to prepare for transitions

"Gradually bring it in until you're riding a centre line. Look ahead of you and start from the corner. If the trot isn't settled ride a circle. Remember to breathe and keep the rhythm."

Carl's first attempt at the centre line isn't straight, Chris says that this was because he wasn't prepared. "Don't do such a tight turn, if you prepare for the turn everything you need should be there." Carl puts this into practice and the next centre line is excellent.

Chris's tip

■ Experiment with riding centre lines from both directions. This way you'll know which is your best rein and you can enter from that direction in your test. When you're riding a test, aim to impress the judge from the very beginning

When you can ride a straight line along the fence, try gradually bringing it to the centre line

THE FINISHING TOUCH

To end the lesson Chris asks Carl to go large and practise riding some halts and move offs. Briar can sometimes be resistant to the hand in downward transitions and this exercise will improve her obedience. Chris explains that Briar hollows when Carl is asking for more engagement. He asks Carl to check that he is using the correct aids. "If you're doing everything right and she's still not listening, you will need to be firmer until she becomes more responsive," he says.

Chris doesn't want Carl to practise halting on the centre line as if he was riding a test. He explains that's it's better to work on getting good halts and move offs elsewhere in the arena and, when these are established, to add them to the centre line movement. This way Briar won't start to anticipate the transition, which could make it more difficult.

When your halts are obedient and straight you're ready to try them on the centre line

Chris's tip

■ If you're working in for a test and having problems halting on the centre line, go away and practise it somewhere else in the arena until your horse is more obedient. When your horse is listening to you, try riding the halt transition on the centre line again

Carl is able to train Briar without relying on Chris to tell him what to do

THE VERDICT

Carl is pleased with Briar today. She can be quite resistant and he feels her attitude is much better. Chris is also very pleased with Carl and Briar's progress. Carl is using his head and Chris says that, by the end of the lesson, he was teaching himself. "Briar was going forward nicely and her stride and outline improved as the lesson went on," says Chris. "She can get a little free at times though so Carl must be careful not to confuse speed with impulsion." Chris comments that Carl's position is good. He needs to watch his reins don't get too long.

Homework

Chris wants Carl to continue the work he has done today. He must remember to warm up properly in walk. It's also important he rides Briar forward in a good rhythm and uses transitions to get her mentally and physically engaged.

Carl needs to think about the quality of Briar's steps. He must also learn to recognise what the good steps feel like. He needs to discipline himself to ride accurate movements in the school.

Take control

Problem: Your horse is strong and fast and cross-country can be a hair-raising experience. You need to learn to ride the approach to each fence and think positively to banish any nerves.

Trainer: Karen Dixon

When riding cross-country there's a fine line between feeling exhilarated and terrified. Cross-country obstacles are unforgiving, so it's important that you have a trusting, positive relationship with your horse. You need to know that your horse has the ability and know-how to jump each fence, and he needs to know that he's got a confident, knowledgeable pilot on board. This relationship will crumble if either horse or rider, or both, are lacking in any of these areas.

Regular cross-country schooling sessions are a must, preferably with an experienced instructor. Having someone on the ground telling you what to do will boost your confidence and a good instructor will turn each lesson into a positive experience.

Ex-racehorse Nessie is typical of many hot-blooded types. She can be fizzy, strong and spooky, which does nothing for Beth's fragile nerves. To make their cross-country performance more consistent and less rushed, Karen had plenty of exercises in mind to steady Nessie's approach, improve her steering and encourage Beth to ride her into each fence.

Beth steadies her approach, keeps a steady contact and clears the fence at the fourth attempt

Beth Hutchinson has owned five-year-old, 15.3hh Thoroughbred Sheer Necessity, or Nessie, for six months. Nessie is an ex-flat racing horse and Beth has taught her to jump from scratch. Nessie is now capable at cross-country, but she can be strong and excitable. The pair compete at Novice level hunter trials. Beth's confidence is easily shaken and Nessie's tendency to take hold and rush at fences doesn't help. Beth tends to panic, brace herself against the horse on the approach to a fence and drop her hands at the last minute. This results in Nessie ducking out, which doesn't help Beth's nerves. She is hoping that Karen will be able to boost her confidence and improve her position.

The lesson

STEADY UP

As Nessie's biggest weak spot is her brakes, Karen is keen to work on her rhythm, especially on the approach to a fence. "You should think rhythm, rhythm all the way," Karen tells Beth. "Approach the fence on a circle, hold a nice, steady contact and give the horse a chance to see the fence."

Beth and Nessie's first fence of the day is a small log, which they clear. The next chair fence, however, brings out the gremlins. Nessie's approach is on the fast side, Beth is slightly hesitant, drops her contact at the last minute and Nessie refuses (pics below). "Don't panic, jump the smaller log and then try again," advises Karen. The log proves no problem, but they have two more refusals at the chair. "Steady your approach and use the left rein to hold Nessie tighter into the fence," says Karen. "You must keep your rein contact consistent. Drop your hands at the last minute and your horse will think that something's not right. That's why she's ducking out." With this in mind, Beth rides Nessie at the fence and clears it.

Below top: Beth drops her contact just before the chair fence and Nessie refuses

Below bottom: Nessie refuses two more times

THE RIGHT APPROACH

Next up is a small course of fences, so it's Beth's job to stick to a rhythm and hold Nessie together. "Because Nessie is strong, every approach to a fence is a fight," says Karen. "Your arms are straight, your body is rigid, you're not relaxed and Nessie is pulling. With strong horses like her the key is to say 'whoa' then relax. So shorten your reins, give one sharp pull, then relax but maintain a contact. When horses are strong, riders tend to just sit there and get carried, when actually it's vital that you use your legs, keep a contact and ride every stride."

Nessie tackles the next two fences well – a beehive and a log – then jumps a sleeper, slows to a trot through a water-logged dip, before jumping up a hill over a pheasant feeder. "Very good," says Karen. "When you take it more slowly, Nessie makes a conscious decision to jump and it's not such a panic."

Karen asks Beth to jump the course the opposite way and Nessie balks at the pheasant feeder and refuses. "Circle away, try again and talk to Nessie as she's obviously a bit uptight," says Karen. At the second attempt, Nessie jumps the course clear and the pair are starting to become more confident (pic below).

Above: Because Nessie is strong, the approach to each fence can turn into a fight

Below: Beth slows her approach to the pheasant feeder and jumps it well

OVER THE DITCH

Next, Karen asks Beth to tackle a ditch. "Approach it on a circle, shorten your reins, stay relaxed and keep a contact," says Karen. Nessie is confident with ditches and jumps first time, though Karen has to remind Beth not to look into the ditch.

"Try again, but this time approach in trot, hold a contact and don't drop your hands over the fence," says Karen. Beth looks up and jumps the ditch nicely (pic below).

COURSES FOR HORSES

All fired up thanks to her success over the ditch, Beth is keen to jump another course of fences. "Jump the beehive, the log, the tiger trap, the ditch, the chair and then the pheasant feeder," Karen tells her. Beth goes clear until the chair fence rears its ugly head again and Nessie puts in one refusal, then another, before clearing it at the third attempt.

"As Nessie has a big jump you tend to collapse your upper body and fall onto her neck over a jump," says Karen. "By tipping your body too far forward and keeping your legs back, you've got no security should the horse stumble or refuse. So sit up, relax your arms and sit as still as possible over the fence." Beth practises this over the small log jump and Karen can see an instant improvement. "Much better," she says. "You might think you need to throw yourself forward to avoid catching Nessie in the mouth, but you've just proven that you can go with

The ditch proves no problem for Nessie

the horse and stay more secure and upright in the saddle."

The next hurdle is a ladder-style fence which Beth and Nessie haven't tried before. It's a straightforward, inviting jump but Nessie spooks and they have a refusal. Beth circles away, makes a more confident approach and they jump it clear. "I could tell Nessie was going to jump that time from three strides out," says Karen. "You were more confident, you drove her at the fence and she responded to your bold approach."

Beth practises sitting as still as possible over the fence

Beth has a tendency to collapse her upper body over a fence

Nessie shows no fear of water as she trots through

Beth and Nessie make an excellent job of jumping into the water...

...and up the bank on the other side

WATER COMPLEX

As Beth and Nessie prepare to tackle a water complex, Karen asks Beth to trot down the ramp and through the water. Nessie shows no sign of fear as she confidently paddles through. "Next, I want you to jump into the water and then jump out over the bank," Karen tells her. "Give the horse a long rein as you jump in, or you'll go straight over her ears if she jumps big. Keep your leg on and allow the horse to look, then maintain a good rein contact through the water." Beth and Nessie make a superb job of the complex and try jumping in off the bigger bank too. They're both feeling confident and it really shows.

With thanks to Sara Metcalfe at the Foxberry Chasers UK Chasers course in Caldwell, Richmond, North Yorkshire. Foxberry Chasers is open for individuals, groups or clubs to use for schooling, clinics and rallies.

Karen Dixon is based nearby and is available for lessons by prior arrangement. This project is supported under the England Rural Development Programme by the Department for Environment, Food and Rural Affairs and the European Agricultural Guidance and Guarantee Fund. For more information contact Sara, tel: 01325 718792.

THE VERDICT

By the end of the lesson it is apparent that when Beth is feeling confident this rubs off on Nessie and the pair's performance improves. As soon as Beth cracks her nerves, her riding becomes much more positive and Nessie takes less of a hold. She's a sensitive horse who will put in a dirty stop the second she feels Beth's contact drop. When Beth relaxes, keeps a consistent contact and rides her into each fence Nessie jumps superbly. However, nerves are a delicate thing, so Beth will benefit from regular lessons to improve her position and gain confidence over different types of fences.

Karen's tip

■ If you're slightly nervous and your horse refuses a fence once or twice, don't keep trying until all confidence is eroded. Go away, jump a smaller, easier fence to boost your nerves and tackle the bogey fence again once you're feeling more together and positive.

Karen's tip

■ Riders often make the mistake of thinking that holding a contact means shortening the reins right up. This encourages you to lean forward. Instead, sit up, relax your arms and maintain a steady contact with the horse's mouth – something I liken to holding a child's hand. If a horse can feel a steady contact, this will build his confidence in the rider

Homework

"Beth needs to work on building both her and Nessie's confidence cross-country before other changes can be implemented," says Karen. "Ideally Beth should ride with shorter stirrups, but if I ask her to do that now it will throw her and she'll feel unsteady in the saddle. As her confidence and position improve, the stirrups can come up a few holes so her lower legs act as a safety belt."

Tailor-made training

Problem: You want your horse to move freely forwards, keeping balanced, supple and straight. These are important basics that you need to achieve if you want your training to progress.

Trainer: Angela Niemeyer

Some of the main aims of schooling a horse are to train him to be calm, willing and obedient. Correct training also enables the horse to do his work to the best of his ability, without stress or strain.

Horses come in all shapes and sizes and they all have different temperaments and abilities. The work we do with them has to be tailored to match these needs. A good trainer will be armed with a whole host of exercises, all designed to achieve specific goals. Lessons can help you to identify your horse's strongest and weakest points and help you build a harmonious and successful relationship.

Walk on a long rein gives the horse a chance to relax and stretch

Mandy Turner has owned eight-year-old William for three years. William is 16.1hh, out of a Clydesdale mare and by Habitat, a top flat racing stallion. He has shown a talent for dressage and the pair compete in affiliated dressage at Elementary level. William has a natural tendency to go on his forehand. Angela says this is simply a result of the way he's built – his back is quite long, he has a powerful well-developed forehand and weaker hindquarters. The aim of today's lesson is to help Mandy to work him correctly. Getting William to carry more weight behind, using the power of his hindlegs to push him forward. Angela wants to show Mandy how to improve William's basic way of going working on his rhythm, speed, suppleness, strength and straightness.

The lesson

GETTING WARMED UP

Angela gives Mandy time to get William properly warmed up and settled in before they start work. She emphasises the importance of doing this. "Warm up your horse on a long rein, just holding the buckle – as long as it's safe. This allows him to really stretch and find his own rhythm, unrestricted and unrestrained." Angela explains that horses need to be allowed to settle down to work on their own, without too much rein, to give them a chance to relax.

Angela watches and points out that William is already slowing down by himself. "If you leave a horse alone he will settle, you don't need to interfere," she says. The warm-up may take around 10 minutes, but the rider shouldn't be afraid to just sit there and do nothing during this time.

William's nose is nicely positioned in front of the vertical and his neck is completely stretched out. Angela says when he's warmed up like this there is no danger of spoiling his natural rhythm and the length of his walk steps.

Angela's tip

■ If you have problems with the regularity of your horse's walk, try riding him over poles as you warm up. Set four poles out about 3' apart, according to your horse's length of stride. Then allow him to walk over them on a long rein. This is a good way of encouraging a regular length of step without any interference from the rider

MOVING ON

After the warm up, Angela asks Mandy to push on into medium walk. "Take a rein contact and give a light nudge with both legs, so you're pushing him forward into both reins." Angela explains that Mandy will also need to give a light seat aid. "Think of it as a slight pelvic thrust – you're opening up the hips and lifting forward but not grinding your seatbones into the saddle or bracing your back."

Angela reminds her that her hands should be positioned in front of the saddle at the base of William's neck. She warns that her hands must not be restrictive. "Follow the horse's movement, don't hold the rein back.

"In medium walk the horse's head should be just in front of the vertical and his poll should be the highest part of his neck. His hind feet should step clearly over the print of his fore feet in a good rhythm. The rein contact is firm but elastic."

Angela asks Mandy to go forward into trot. She reminds her that whenever she picks up the rein she first needs to use a forward aid. This is so you never pull the horse in from the front. "If you pull him in you'll block his back and hindlegs and will restrict his movement."

WORK IN TROT

Angela concentrates on getting the trot forward and in the correct rhythm. Mandy is working in rising trot and Angela says

Mandy uses her inside leg, making sure she has a steady contact in her outside rein, to get William working nicely on the circle

she should adjust the speed by applying half-halts from time to time as she sits. "As you sit, close your legs against the horse's sides and push him into a closed hand and then allow," she explains.

Angela is happy with the trot and asks Mandy to bring William onto a circle so they can start to work him in a deeper outline. To do this Mandy will have to take a little more contact in her outside rein and use plenty of inside leg.

Angela explains that all horses are naturally crooked to varying degrees. "I have found that most, if not all, horses find it easier to bend to the left," she says. "As the neck bends left, the right hindleg will move to the right, creating a distinct S-bend through the horse's body."

In order to help improve William's straightness Angela tells Mandy not to ask for left neck bend while she is on the left rein. "It's better to ride him straight at times on the left rein, even flex him a little to the outside until he accepts the outside rein," she explains.

Mandy pushes William on into medium walk

Angela's tips

■ You will know your horse is accepting the outside rein when his neck fills the space against the outside rein and looks hollow on the inside. If he is carrying himself you can give the reins briefly forward and he will stay in the same outline and at the same speed.

■ To know what degree of bend you're aiming for on a circle, imagine drawing in the line of the circle under your horse's body. If you were to do this he would have a fore and a hindleg positioned on either side of the line, so the hind feet should be following in the tracks of the fore feet.

Crookedness makes it
difficult for the horse to
step under his body

Transitions within the pace are a useful exercise

Give and retake the reins to check for self-carriage

FINE-TUNING

Angela thinks William and Mandy are doing well. She reminds Mandy that if he starts to fall in on the circle she must think of using a leg-yielding aid to push him back out and vice versa.

Now she asks Mandy to ride some transitions within the trot. To do this she will need to use half-halts. Angela explains that this is a good way of introducing young horses to collection. "To get a horse supple it's just as important to ride transitions in the same pace as it is to ride transitions to other paces," she says.

Angela explains that during the exercise Mandy's seat will come more into the saddle, her leg is briefly holding, and her rein briefly restraining. This brings the horse back without losing the momentum. She should then ride forward again. "This gets the horse used to collecting and going forward," says Angela. "The exercise is good for the hindlegs, making the horse more able to take the weight on his haunches. The aim is to help the horse and rider to carry themselves better."

Angela reminds Mandy not to have too much inside neck bend when she's on the left rein and too little when she's on the right. "On the right rein, work on making the contact more even. Remember he has no natural right bend so make sure he's flexed right. You should just be able to see his inside eye on both reins."

Mandy starts to feel that William is getting more supple and easier in the rein. He is bending to the right now without her having to hold him there. To test this she gives the right rein forward.

Angela's tip

■ When leg-yielding the aim is to move the horse forwards and sideways, away from your inside leg toward the outside. The horse's head is always positioned slightly away from the direction of the movement. The inside leg is placed on or just behind the girth (depending on the horse's training). The outside leg is behind the girth, repeating the aids as necessary, asking rather than pushing tightly.

CANTER WORK

Angela asks Mandy to try some canter on the left rein. She gets her to flex William's neck to the outside. Angela explains that the purpose of this is to position his hindlegs to the left, making him straighter and allowing him to step more underneath his body.

When William is straighter in his body Mandy can ask for more inside bend. To check that he's carrying himself Angela gets Mandy to give and retake the reins. She's pleased to see that William maintains the same rhythm and outline.

As they change the rein, Angela reminds Mandy to think of the canter as being uphill. "The canter should maintain its three beats – never slowing to four beats," she says.

Angela is using exercises to strengthen William's hindlegs so he becomes stronger behind. He has worked hard and she doesn't want him to get tight in his back. "Allow him to stretch more forward now," she says. Angela comments that William's canter is improving, he is naturally sitting more and Mandy is finding him easier to sit to.

Angela asks Mandy to go large then, from the centre line, leg yield to the track. She's looking for the horse to remain straight, moving forwards and sideways, keeping the rhythm in the canter. Mandy must be sure his outside shoulder doesn't come over too much or that his quarters start to lead.

It's helpful to have someone watching you when you're learning to leg-yield

FINISHING OFF

As a final exercise Angela asks Mandy to turn up the quarter lines of the school and ride a long, thin rectangle in canter. "When you can do this try turning it into a square," she says. "To ride the turns you will first need to turn him using your weight to the inside and your inside leg. Your outside rein will go towards his neck and the inside rein will come slightly away from the neck to show him where to go. The outside leg stays in canter position to dictate the tightness of the turn," she explains.

Angela adds that this is a difficult exercise for both horse and rider to master, but it's useful for working on collection, getting the horse to sit and improving the canter.

William has worked hard and it's time to let him stretch and cool down. Angela believes it's just as important to cool off as it is to warm up. "The horse should go back to the stables cool and calm."

THE VERDICT

Angela says it's important to see how a horse reacts to the work he's doing. William isn't sweating heavily after today's lesson so he has not been overstretched. This shows he is capable of doing such strenuous work.

Angela is happy with William's progress. He is going really well and doing the basic work very nicely. To continue improving she thinks he needs to do a lot of strengthening work and more of the type of work he did today to encourage him to carry less weight on his forehand. Mandy is very pleased with the lesson. She found some of the exercises quite difficult but thought William felt much better as the lesson progressed.

William has coped well with Angela's exercises

Quarter turns can be difficult

■ Please note that the type of riding hat used in this lesson can legally be worn in dressage competitions. Although we would recommend always riding in a hat with a correctly fitting harness, its use is a matter of personal choice.

Homework

Angela says Mandy needs to do more of the same work that they did today. She'll need to keep on doing strengthening exercises with William – plenty of work in canter will be good for this.

Angela says the canter work will also help to improve the trot. She points out that William's gaskin (second thigh) could be more developed and this work will hopefully help.

Frustrated ambitions

Problem: Nerves are seriously hampering your cross-country progress, but you're desperate to improve and compete in a hunter trial.

Trainer: Karen Dixon

Most riders will admit to butterflies in their stomach at the thought of a potentially worrying situation, but when nerves really take a hold they can severely hamper your riding progress. That's the problem faced by Donna Wood and her horse Shaddy. Donna is a competent rider with a willing, sensible horse and she's desperate to compete in a hunter trial. However, her nerves are proving a barrier.

Donna is hesitant on the approach to a fence and fails to maintain a contact. Shaddy loses impulsion and rhythm and either refuses or cat leaps the fence. Donna gets left behind and jabs him in the mouth, which damages his confidence and makes him more reluctant to jump next time. It's a vicious circle.

Once Donna cracks her nerves, ups the pace and really rides Shaddy into each fence, a talented rider emerges and their performance improves. It's finding and maintaining this confident approach that's the key.

Donna Wood runs a livery yard and has owned Arctic Shadow, or Shaddy, for three years. Shaddy, a seven-year-old, 16.1hh Connemara x Thoroughbred is a laid-back character, although he can be strong. Donna bought Shaddy after a long break from riding and is a nervous, hesitant rider. She has regular cross-country lessons and it is her ambition to compete in a hunter trial. With Karen's help, Donna is determined to crack the problem of her nerves. Shaddy often puts in a refusal at the first fence, due to a lack of impulsion and rhythm. Karen hopes to encourage Donna to maintain a contact, move with the horse and stop worrying so much.

The lesson

GETTING LEFT BEHIND

When Donna and Shaddy have worked in on the flat, Karen asks Donna to pop over a small upright, approaching in trot on a circle. They jump clear in both directions, but Karen is keen to see more rein contact. "Improve your contact, but don't simply shorten the reins," she explains. "I liken maintaining a contact to holding a horse's hand. Your horse will gain confidence if you hold his hand and guide him over the fence. Without a contact he'll be lost and worried, so take up the reins and position your hands over the neck strap of the breastplate."

With the warm-up fence safely negotiated, Karen asks Donna to canter down a slope, through a large puddle and up the bank on the other side, jumping out over a pheasant feeder. Shaddy lacks impulsion on the approach to the fence, cat leaps and Donna gets left behind (pics above). When the same thing happens a second time, Karen pulls them up. "Every time the horse cat leaps and you get left behind the movement, you accidentally catch him in the teeth because you're unbalanced and your reins are too short," says Karen. She would prefer Donna to use D-rings on her pelham in the future, rather than a single rein on the bottom ring, and remove the curb chain to make things easier on Shaddy's mouth. However, Donna is afraid she'll lose control, so they decide to leave things as they are for this lesson.

"You're worrying too much and it's not doing you any favours," says Karen. She suggests some adjustments in Donna's position, which should make her more secure and help her confidence. "Keep your weight in your stirrups, rather than gripping with your knees, and bring your bottom further back in the saddle. At the moment you are behind the movement and going against the horse. Stand in the stirrups slightly and keep your weight in your feet. This will improve your balance and you'll automatically find yourself moving with the horse."

Donna takes on board Karen's advice, circles away, gets up some speed and makes a much tidier job of jumping the pheasant feeder. This boosts her confidence, ready for the next set of jumps.

Shaddy lacks impulsion on the approach to the pheasant feeder, cat leaps and Donna gets left behind

Donna increases her impulsion and maintains a contact on the approach. The result is a better jump

THREE OF A KIND

Next are two log jumps, followed by a sleeper fence. Donna manages to hold her nerve over the logs and clears them both first time. She now looks far more confident, picking up the pace and going with the horse's movement. However, Donna's gremlins reappear at the sleeper fence, she drops the contact and they have two refusals, clearing it at the third attempt.

"You must maintain a consistent contact with Shaddy's mouth. This is essential so that when you need to steer him towards a fence, a feel on the reins doesn't come as such a shock to him," advises Karen.

Donna shows improvement over the first log fence

Donna drops the contact on the approach to the sleeper and they have a refusal

They clear it at the third attempt

DITCH IT

As Karen asks the pair to move on to the next set of fences, Donna has her reservations about the first obstacle, a ditch. Donna is a hesitant rider and potentially spooky obstacles, such as this ditch, require a confident, rhythmic approach.

"Go, go, go!" Karen shouts as Donna makes her third attempt, following two refusals. Shaddy refuses for a third time and, on his next attempt, stumbles into the ditch, instead of taking off over it.

"You need to hold Shaddy together so he knows it's a team effort," explains Karen. "Pick up the pace, steer him towards the ditch, maintain a contact and you'll give him the confidence to jump." Donna shortens her reins, keeps her legs on and Shaddy jumps the ditch at the fifth try, albeit clumsily. Donna gets left behind the movement, but at least they are over.

"Your reins were a little too short," says Karen. "Holding a contact doesn't mean shortening the reins, as this will encourage you to lean forward and lose your balance. Sit up, relax your arms and keep a consistent feel with your horse's mouth.

"When you get your speed up and inject some adrenalin into your riding, you do so much better. Attack the ditch this time."

Donna's nerves melt away as she approaches the ditch. She rides forward from the leg, keeps a good contact and Shaddy jumps well.

"Maintain the impulsion towards the next fence and show some aggression," says Karen as Donna approaches a small upright. Shaddy clears the upright but refuses at the pheasant feeder, eventually jumping it at the third attempt.

Donna picks up the pace, holds Shaddy together and steers him towards the ditch. They clear it clumsily

A much better attempt. Donna maintains a contact and jumps the ditch well

An uncertain approach to the ditch results in several refusals

GOING PLACES

"As Donna tackles the final set of fences, there's a big improvement in her riding and approach to each jump. She's feeling positive, pushing Shaddy on and making an effort to go with his movement over each fence. First she jumps clear over a telegraph pole, then pops over the ditch and finally clears a tiger trap.

Karen asks Donna to attempt the three fences again and, despite getting in close to the tiger trap, she clears them all.

"Fantastic! What a big improvement," says Karen. "Just see the difference when you stop worrying and ride forwards positively."

Donna's reins are still too short, but a more positive approach gives Shaddy the confidence to clear the final set of fences

Homework

Hopefully, as Donna's confidence increases with practice, she will no longer get left behind Shaddy's movement and catch him in the teeth.

Not many horses will continue to jump when it causes them pain, so Donna should look at switching to a milder bit or using D-rings on the pelham.

It is impossible to suddenly become confident overnight, it's a slow process. Donna should have regular lessons and aim for steady progress.

Karen is sure Donna will be able to compete in a hunter trial, but she must learn to maintain a rhythmic, balanced pace, move with her horse and get that adrenalin working positively

THE VERDICT

Donna's confidence is easily shaken. However, as the lesson progresses, her riding improves. Shaddy's confidence increases with a good approach and Donna finds it easier to balance in the saddle when she establishes a forward-going, rhythmic canter.

If Donna is to have any chance of competing, she needs regular lessons and practice sessions to help conquer her nerves. She should focus on the high she gets when she clears a fence successfully. "At this stage, when schooling at home, Donna shouldn't try anything too big or technical. She needs to focus her energy on riding positively towards each fence, rather than worrying," advises Karen.

Plan of action

Problem: You and your horse are competent over jumps, but your horse is prone to the occasional stop. You need to go back to basics to formulate a plan of action to prevent this.

Trainer: Mia Korenika

If you have ever ridden confidently into the show jumping ring, only to falter half way round, it is likely that you will have felt all that hard–won confidence slipping away. A stop or run out can shatter your nerves and damage your trust in your horse.

This is a familiar scenario for Tish Billett and her horse Foxy Lady, who compete in unaffiliated show jumping classes. Foxy is prone to refusing and one mistake like this will often throw their whole performance, as Tish gets flustered and her confidence ebbs away.

Tish needs to concentrate on her flatwork to make sure she is riding Foxy effectively and giving her every chance to jump in a balanced, rhythmical way. She also needs to try some gridwork exercises to improve her confidence, regain her trust in Foxy and formulate a plan of action to avoid mishaps. A confident approach will help her cope when things go wrong. If Tish can keep her cool around a course of jumps, she and Foxy will be a winning combination.

Tish Billett has owned Foxy Lady, a 16.1hh, nine–year–old ID x TB for five years. The pair compete in Preliminary dressage and unaffiliated show jumping classes. Foxy was hand reared as a foal and, as a result, can be overconfident and disrespectful of her rider, both when being handled on the ground and when ridden.

Tish hopes Mia will be able to give her some advice on coping with Foxy's devious streak. Foxy throws in the occasional dirty stop while jumping as soon as she feels Tish weaken her contact, and one mistake like this knocks Tish's confidence, especially at a show. Tish needs to go back to basics with her flatwork. Then it's time for some gridwork exercises to build Tish's confidence and make Foxy's performance more consistent.

The lesson

Mia asks Tish to soften her elbows and relax her hands and legs

Tish and Foxy ride two, half 10-metre circles, which teaches co-ordination and obedience

WORKING IN

As Tish and Foxy work in on the flat, Mia watches to see how the horse moves and responds to Tish's aids. It is vital that both horse and rider are working effectively on the flat before they start to jump, and getting the basics right is especially important if your horse is prone to refusing. A devious horse will take advantage of any rider weakness, so Mia is keen to see Tish relaxed, confident and in control at all paces.

Mia asks Tish to make some subtle improvements to her position. "Keep your thumbs on top, soften your elbows, relax your hands and legs and aim to stay in balance with the horse," says Mia. "On a scale of one to 10, imagine that your leg pressure on the horse's sides is around the two mark."

To maintain a steady contact on the outside rein, Mia asks Tish to position her outside hand on the horse's neck in all paces. She says this is a useful, simple schooling exercise for riders who find it tricky to keep a stable contact, as it gives them a feel for where their outside hand should be.

SUPPLE UP

Once Foxy has loosened up, the first flatwork exercise uses two, half 10-metre circles, changing the direction each time. This will encourage Foxy to move away from the leg and engage her hindquarters (see the panel below left for more on this). This is a useful exercise for both Tish and Foxy. From the rider's point of view, the exercise helps to develop co-ordination of the aids, as seat, leg and hand aids must be used together. It also teaches the rider to use one leg independently of the other and encourages the horse to stay between hand and leg. This exercise will get Foxy listening to Tish and more obedient to the leg. It will increase her suppleness and make her more responsive to the aids, encouraging her to engage her quarters and bring her hindleg through and underneath herself.

This type of exercise will benefit Tish and encourage her to really ride a course of jumps, rather than being a passenger. If Tish can sharpen up Foxy and get her listening and responding to the aids before she starts jumping, she will be less likely to refuse when they do tackle fences.

Riding two, half 10-metre circles:

■ As you walk down the long side, collect the walk and turn in slightly from the outside track, remaining parallel to the track

■ Ride a half 10-metre circle right

■ Ride two strides straight to balance the horse, before reapplying the aids for a half 10-metre circle left. Then rejoin the track

■ Riding two, half 10-metre circles requires concentration and precise aids. Throughout this exercise, use your inside leg to your outside rein and stabilise the outside contact

■ This exercise encourages the horse to step through and underneath with his inside hindleg, therefore engaging the quarters. It also helps to improve the horse's balance and suppleness and helps with the rider's co-ordination of the aids

WORKING ON TRANSITIONS

Foxy can be hesitant and drop behind the bridle, resisting the contact, so Mia asks Tish to work on sharpening Foxy's walk-to-trot transitions while working on a circle. "Think of your transitions as a flick of a light switch: squeeze and expect to get an answer," says Mia.

"While riding on a circle, use your inside leg to create the bend, squeeze the inside rein and keep a steady contact on the outside rein. Allow your lower leg to drop and relax – if you stop gripping with your calves your horse will work in a better rhythm – and keep thinking 'inside leg to outside rein'.

"The aids for a downwards transition are virtually the same as those for a half-halt (see panel below left), so keep practising your walk-to-trot and trot-to-walk transitions."

As Tish and Foxy progress to walk-to-canter transitions, Tish loses the contact repeatedly so Mia asks her to shorten the reins and sit up on her seat bones. To encourage Tish to sit deeper in the saddle, Mia asks her to canter on a circle and lift her legs off the saddle for two strides and then put them back again. This is a difficult exercise and, although Tish struggles with it, she can really feel her seat bones beneath her.

Another exercise Mia suggests to help Tish remain balanced is to sit deep for two strides of trot and then stand in the stirrups for two strides, then repeat this exercise in canter. This deep seat/light seat exercise is ideal for Tish, who finds it difficult to maintain a contact while adopting a lighter seat and can get ahead of Foxy's movement.

"These flatwork exercises work to get horse and rider thinking and test the rider's co-ordination," says Mia. "When Tish jumps it is vital that all the necessary buttons are working so Foxy listens to her aids and responds instantly."

The aids for a half-halt/downwards transition:

■ Grow tall through your spine
■ Close your fingers on the rein to contain the horse's forward movement, so he becomes more collected
■ Relax your legs
■ The horse will briefly pause in his forward movement, becoming contained by the rein aids (for a downwards transition), before you apply your legs again to ask for a forward movement (for a half-halt)

Tish loses the contact in walk-to-canter transitions, so Mia asks her to shorten the reins and sit up

Mia asks Tish to sit for two strides of trot...

...then rise for two strides

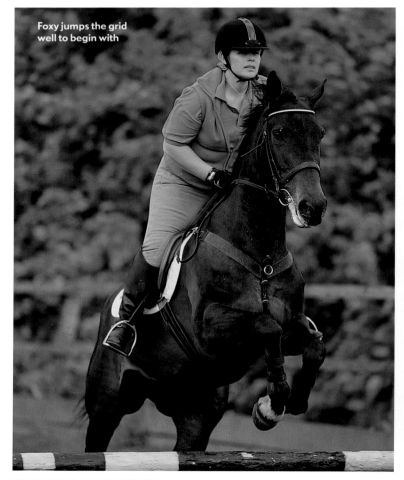

Foxy jumps the grid well to begin with

She refuses three times in a row when the upright is raised by a few inches

With the ground poles removed, Tish jumps the upright at the second attempt, getting left behind when Foxy jumps big

TIME FOR GRIDWORK

With the flatwork session over, it is time for some gridwork. "Grids discipline the horse to accept the contact on the approach to a fence, over the jump and on landing. This improves the horse and rider's confidence," says Mia as she sets up a pole 10-12m before a small upright, with another pole 10-12m after the fence. "Halt before the pole, step over it, then make a snappy walk-to-canter transition, pop the fence, and walk over the final pole."

Tish and Foxy clear the grid, but Foxy bounds into canter and jumps the fence too fast. Mia asks Tish to maintain a contact, steady her approach and try again. They jump it better this time, but when Mia raises the upright by a few inches Foxy takes advantage of Tish's slight apprehension. The mare refuses three times in a row, eventually jumping it at the fourth attempt.

"Foxy will often drop behind the bridle a couple of strides before the fence and Tish is too trusting," says Mia. "She releases the contact slightly and Foxy takes advantage of this and puts in a sneaky stop. As soon as Foxy refuses, Tish's confidence takes a knock. Her legs swing back, she tips forward and her position becomes unbalanced.

"Instead of falling to pieces when things go wrong, Tish must be quick to pick up where she left off. She needs to remember everything we've done on the flat and put it into practice. Foxy should be responsive to the aids and moving forwards with rhythm and balance. She should make snappy transitions and move away from the leg. If Tish can maintain a contact and guide Foxy over each fence, she will respond. She'll only stop when she knows she can get away with it."

Once Foxy has cleared the upright a couple of times and Tish has regained her confidence, Mia takes away the poles and asks Tish to approach the upright in canter. She should apply the same principles she used when the poles were there – maintaining a contact and steady rhythm.

Foxy refuses at the first attempt, jumps big the second time but finally gets it right on the third go.

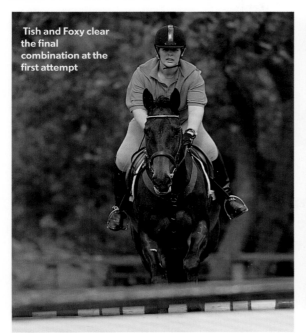

Tish and Foxy clear the final combination at the first attempt

JUMP TO IT

Next, Mia sets up two fences to be jumped in a straight line across the school. "Make a definite turn, come in straight from the corner, maintain a bouncy, rhythmic canter and aim for three good strides between the fences," says Mia. "Sit up, get your balance and remember all that work we did on the flat. Close your fingers around the reins, maintain a contact and use your seat."

Tish and Foxy jump clear first time, but Tish has to ride strongly through the combination. "Great, but you're doing all the work," says Mia. "You need a bigger, better canter." Foxy jumps clear a second, third and fourth time and Tish ends the lesson on a high. "That was much better," says Mia. "When you hold a contact, ride forwards and guide Foxy over each fence she doesn't think about stopping."

THE VERDICT

Thanks to Mia's help, Tish manages to improve Foxy's way of going on the flat. Foxy is more supple, responsive and energetic by the end of the first half of the lesson. Once Tish remembers to put all her schooling work into practice when riding over fences, her performance improves and so does her confidence. Tish is pleased with what she and Foxy have achieved in just an hour and is planning more lessons to build on this.

Homework

"Even though Tish and Foxy are both experienced, they need to work on the basics," says Mia. "Regular flatwork sessions are important as it's vital that a safe, effective way of riding is second nature. If something does go wrong and Foxy refuses, Tish needs the ability and confidence to recover, learn from the experience and carry on.

"Tish shouldn't jump anything too big or technical at this stage, as she needs to continue with the gridwork. Varied gridwork can improve control and encourage Tish not to panic when Foxy thinks about running out. Instead, she should sit up, keep a contact and maintain that all-important rhythm."

Getting engaged

Problem: You want your horse to work through his back into a soft, even contact so that he becomes easier to ride and more obedient to your aids.

Trainer: Angela Niemeyer

The lesson
Riding corners

You only need to look at the track in an arena to see that most of us do not ride into the corners. This simple movement, if ridden correctly, will activate your horse's hindlegs, particularly the inside hindleg, which helps improve engagement and power.

As you ride towards the corner in walk, put your inside leg on at the girth. Move your outside leg back, but don't just move it from the knee, try to move the whole leg from the hip as this will automatically place more weight onto your inside seatbone. Position your inside shoulder back and your outside shoulder a little forward, in line with your horse's shoulders and the line of the corner. In walk, the deepest part of the corner should be 3m from the edge of the school (this changes as the paces increase – it would be too deep for trot or canter).

On the first attempt, Angela notices that Cathy needs to raise her outside shoulder a little while dropping her inside shoulder slightly so that her weight comes onto the inside seatbone. Also, she needs to put her inside leg on the girth more definitely to ask Pye to bend round it. In the pic right we can

Cathy Lammie has owned Pye for seven months. Pye is a 16.1hh mare by Criminal Law out of a Paint Horse mare. Cathy is an experienced rider and has already seen some improvement in Pye's schooling. She still finds it a little tricky to get Pye to work through from behind and Pye has a tendency to lean on the right rein, which makes it difficult to turn and flex her in that direction. The aim of the lesson is to give Cathy some exercises she can incorporate into her schooling sessions. She wants to help Pye become softer in the right rein and more engaged behind.

already see that Pye is engaged behind and Cathy comments that she has more feel in the outside rein.

Angela says, "Squeeze the inside rein. Close the fingers tighter for a moment to encourage her to flex to the inside. If she doesn't respond, turn your wrist inward slightly as if you are turning a door knob, then give. Follow the horse's movement with your outside rein but don't give it away or she will run out through her outside shoulder. As you ride out of the corner, straighten Pye by reducing the inside flexion, and make sure that both legs are on the girth and that you are sitting in a central and straight position."

ENGAGEMENT AND IMPULSION

Impulsion is the power that comes from the hindquarters. If this power is not harnessed by the proper engagement of the hindlegs and transmitted over a soft, round back into a submissive contact, then a horse's true potential will not be realised. All the work we do is focused on finding ways to engage the hindlegs, particularly the inside hindleg so the horse steps under his centre of gravity and accepts more weight through flexion of the joints of the hindleg. This helps improve the horse's balance, encourages him to be lighter on the forehand, develops self-carriage and increases suppleness. This in turn will lead to collection.

Angela's tip

■ Corners, serpentines, circles and transitions will all help your horse to engage his hindlegs

TRANSITIONS

Transitions are important and are central to improving the way your horse goes. Angela starts by asking Cathy to ride a trot-to-walk transition. On her first attempt, Cathy's body falls forward, she uses too much hand and produces an untidy transition. Angela runs through the aids with Cathy before she tries the exercise again.

Transition recipe

You need to find out, by trial and error, how much of each ingredient you need for your particular horse.
1 Go into sitting trot, riding the horse forward
2 Use your body – push your stomach out slightly, put more weight into your seatbones and sit up. By slowing down your own body movement, your horse will respond to you and much less rein will be needed to complete the transition
3 Take and then give the outside rein to back up the weight aid

SITTING TROT

As Angela asks Cathy to ride an exercise in sitting trot, it is clear that Cathy is not comfortable and she comments that she finds it difficult to sit to Pye's trot. Angela picks up on a few areas of Cathy's position that are causing her problems. Angela feels that Cathy may be using the wrong muscles to try to stay in the saddle. Pye has a lovely active trot and it should be easy to sit to. Cathy needs to push out her stomach slightly and bring her shoulders back so that she sits more upright and imagines herself sinking into the saddle, relaxing her bottom and sitting definitely into the saddle. Her legs should not be tight against the horse – she should let them hug Pye's sides softly without nudging all the time. After Cathy's position has been altered, she looks more comfortable and Pye is really swinging in her back. Cathy will need to work on this at home.

Walk-to-halt transition

Angela asks Cathy to try a walk-to-halt transition. At the first attempt, Pye hollows away from Cathy's seat aids, so Cathy needs to be a little more tactful. It is important not to grind the seatbones into the saddle – the uncomfortable pressure will cause the horse to dip his back. After a few more attempts, Pye comes into a square halt with her hindlegs more underneath her (pic above). Cathy feels Pye is really responding to her weight and becoming much softer in her hand.

Private Lessons

HELPING HANDS

Angela notices that Cathy opens her fingers around the reins. She says this is a common fault which usually occurs when the rider is trying to make the contact lighter. Try this for a softer feel (pic top right): Pass the rein between the index finger and a flat thumb, with the thumb uppermost and pointing towards the horse's ears. Close the ring finger first and then softly close the other fingers around the rein. This hand position, in conjunction with a soft wrist, bent elbow (pic above), relaxed shoulders, and a correct position in the saddle, will achieve the necessary elasticity in the contact. A straight arm gives the horse a rigid contact and he won't want to go into the rein.

LOVELY LEGS

Angela reminds Cathy that her legs should apply a light, even pressure all the way down their length, and not just stay jammed on at the bottom, with the heels pressing into the horse's side. Cathy's lower leg is too constant and strong. Angela asks her to take her feet out of the stirrups. She checks how Cathy uses her outside leg and reminds Cathy that it should go back from the hip not from the knee. Cathy needs to work on loosening her legs and becoming more aware of where her hips are in relation to her position. Angela suggests she should ride without stirrups, lifting her thighs off the saddle and holding that position for a few seconds. Cathy can slowly build up this until she is able to loosen her leg contact at will.

Angela also comments that it is essential not to keep kicking all the time as this decreases the horse's sensitivity to the leg aids. One aid, backed up if necessary by a tap of the whip, should be all that is needed for the horse to go forward. This is then repeated when necessary to keep the horse alert. Between aids the rider should sit quietly.

94

PUTTING IT INTO PRACTICE

To test what Cathy has learned, Angela asks her to ride down the long side of the school in working trot, shorten Pye's steps by the use of her body, then ride a transition into walk and finally free walk on a long rein. This puts into practice all that Cathy has already done and really tests whether Pye is listening. Cathy repeats the exercise several times. Although she is pleased with Pye's progress, she feels that Pye is still leaning on the right rein. Angela encourages her to keep the contact on the right rein and use her left leg to push the horse to the right.

Cathy has come full circle, back to the corner exercise that she used at the beginning of the session. To build on this, Angela asks Cathy to ride a small circle in the corner of the school in walk and, as she comes out of the circle, to continue up the long side of the school.

At this stage, Angela wants Cathy to keep Pye's neck straight but bring the shoulders off the track. This is the beginning of shoulder-in (see panel right). Angela says, "Imagine that you're going to turn across the school, so prepare the aids for a turn but, instead, keep riding straight on."

Cathy rides the shoulder-in a few more times, but without asking for flexion in the neck. This is to test that Pye has truly moved her shoulders, rather than just bending in her neck and leaving her shoulders on the track. Angela comments that Cathy tends to give away the outside rein and loses control of Pye's shoulders. She should ride with the outside rein a fraction longer so she can bend her elbow and keep it by her side. This way she should be able to control the shoulders more. It is vital that the shoulders come off the track and the quarters don't drift out.

Angela's tip
■ Try any new exercises in walk first before moving up a pace

THE VERDICT

Angela feels that getting Cathy to become more aware of her position has improved her weight aids, contact and feel. Riding better transitions, corners, circles and serpentines has helped Pye's balance, rhythm and suppleness and Cathy has found Pye easier to ride.

Cathy feels that Angela tuned into the problems she was having and gave her exercises that helped. Pye was listening more and really responded to her weight aids. By the end of the session she felt much softer in the right rein. Cathy knows she must focus on her own position which will, in turn, help Pye to go better. She will work on this in future lessons with Angela.

Homework
Cathy needs to pay more attention to improving straightness and suppleness.
She should continue with the exercises used in the lesson so that Pye becomes more obedient to the inside leg, the outside rein and works more softly over her back.

Ditch it!

Problem: The horse you ride has problems at ditches. You want to get him jumping them confidently before your first competition.

Trainer: Jeanette Brakewell

If you are planning to compete at cross–country, you are bound to come across a variety of fences which include a ditch in some shape or form. Ditches are well known for causing difficulties, usually because the rider is tempted to look down into the ditch and this makes her nervous. The fear transmits to the horse and can cause him to become wary of this type of fence. The secret to jumping ditches is to keep looking up and ahead so your cross–country rounds become trouble free.

Caroline Lewis rides Anna for her owner Lynn. Anna is a six-year-old TB mare. Last year the pair competed at riding club level, and they plan to do their first pre-novice event in May.

Caroline hopes Jeanette will be able to help them become confident jumping ditches. Anna has been nappy and sometimes a little unco-operative in the past, but she is a talented jumper. They need to practise over the various ditch-type fences they may come across when competing, so they can grow in confidence together.

The lesson

AN EFFECTIVE POSITION

After warming up over some little log fences, Jeanette makes a few alterations to Caroline's position. She asks Caroline to adopt more of a show jumping position by sitting up and keeping her shoulders back as she approaches the fence. She feels Caroline's shoulders are a little too far forward. In this position, if Anna puts in a short stride before take-off, Caroline is already forward and this makes the jump feel uncomfortable. Also, she is not in an effective position to ride Anna forward if she backs off from the fence.

Jeanette tells Caroline to sit up with her shoulders back about five or six strides away from the fence, to soften her arms a little and to remember to keep the canter more forward. She should also think of her knee being soft as this will help her lower leg stay more secure and effective. After a few more jumps, Jeanette says the rhythm is becoming better and Caroline's position is also improving. She just needs to shorten the reins slightly and let her arms become longer, as her elbow is still a little fixed by her side.

START SIMPLE

Jeanette asks Caroline to start with a simple sloping rail fence with a ditch underneath. It is not too big and has a good straight approach. The bottom rail is set low to the ground almost hiding the ditch, so this should help Caroline and Anna to jump it more confidently. Jeanette is quick to reassure Caroline, "Don't ride this fence any differently from the others. Don't think 'will she?', think 'she will!'" Anna and Caroline approach the fence in a good canter and jump it well.

Jeanette reminds Caroline to let Anna use her head and neck as she jumps because she looks a little restricted over the fence. "Allowing your arms forward will help Anna use herself more. Keep your arms soft and allow with the contact to free her head and neck over the fences," she explains.

Sloping rails with ditch underneath

■ This is a relatively easy introduction to ditch fences. The rails form an ascending spread, making it easier to judge and jump. As long as the first rail is close to the floor and the majority of the ditch is covered up, the horse has no idea there is a ditch there at all

■ You should approach this fence with plenty of impulsion, so that if your horse backs off a little he will still have enough energy to jump it. Building up your horse's confidence over this type of fence will reap rewards when you come to negotiate more complex ditch fences

Moving on up

Next Jeanette asks Caroline to jump a plain ditch, approached on a downhill slope. Anna grinds to a halt (pic 1). Jeanette tells Caroline to keep using her legs – she notices that Caroline is using her hands well to keep Anna as straight as possible on the approach, but as Anna moves forward to jump the ditch Caroline stops using her legs (pic 2). Jeanette says, "You are sending mixed messages. You are telling her to go forwards but the moment she goes to do that you take your legs off and she wonders what's wrong." Eventually, Anna clears the ditch (pic 3), and Jeanette asks Caroline to jump it several times in both directions so that Anna becomes more confident.

Plain ditch

The sooner a young horse is introduced to ditches the better, as long as he has enough basic education to go forward when asked and stay straight.

■ A small natural ditch is often more appealing for your horse to jump than a man-made, lined ditch which can look a little spooky

■ Keep your eyes forward and focused on the landing side; don't be tempted to look down into the ditch

■ Imagine you are negotiating a spread fence, increasing the impulsion as you get closer to the fence (ask for a bolder trot or even a few strides of canter just before take-off). Eventually, as your horse's confidence grows, you can approach in a controlled canter

INTRODUCING DITCH COMBINATIONS

The next fence is a coffin combination, approached downhill. There is a set of rails in, one stride to the ditch, then another stride to the rails out. Because of the sloping ground, Jeanette tells Caroline that she will need to be steady on the approach, as it may be slippery, but the canter must be going forward – otherwise she will not have enough impulsion to negotiate the rails. On their first attempt Caroline is sending mixed messages to Anna by pushing her forwards and then restricting with her hand, which results in a refusal (pic above left). Jeanette says, "You're saying 'stop', you must continue to use your legs, but also allow with your hands. Go round the first element and jump the ditch on its own." Anna pops over the ditch nicely.

On the second attempt their approach is better and Anna really uses her neck over the rails (pic above right). Caroline rides positively all the way through. Jeanette says, "Next time trust her, don't harass her, sit a little quieter but still use your legs to make her go forwards. Don't be tempted to use your seat too hard as this will make her hollow."

Coffin fence (rail-ditch-rail)

A coffin fence usually consists of three elements: the first fence is usually rails, followed by a ditch and then another set of rails. A lot of cross-country courses include a rail-ditch-rail combination, and it is used to test your ability to approach in balance, with sufficient impulsion and at the correct speed. This type of fence also tests the horse's boldness, agility and confidence. The degree of difficulty is dictated by:

■ The siting of the fence
■ The steepness of the slope on either side of the ditch
■ The distance between the rails and the ditch
■ The dimensions of the ditch
■ The height of the rails
■ The going

When introducing a horse to this type of fence for the first time it is best to do it in three stages:

1 Pop over the ditch on its own
2 Then jump the ditch and the rail out
3 Finally, put all three elements together

Only move on to the next stage when your horse is confidently popping over the elements in the previous stage.

Your approach is very important. The horse must be in balance and straight, and you should not approach too fast as the first element may hide the ditch. Approach in a good bouncy canter with impulsion so your horse will find it easy to jump.

The rider's position is also important – you should not get ahead of the movement on the approach. Stay soft in the knee so your lower leg is secure, let your horse do the work and wait for him to take off before folding forwards. If anything does go wrong you are in a secure position and you can ride forwards positively. Always look up and ahead, don't be tempted to look down into the ditch.

Jeanette asks Caroline to ride through the combination again. They jump the ditch nicely and then ride out of the final set of rails.

Although Jeanette thinks Caroline's position is getting better, she must keep reminding herself to relax her arms. This will allow Anna to stretch her head and neck. The more freedom Anna has in her head and neck, the easier she will be able to jump the fences. Jeanette says it is not always easy to change ingrained habits, so Caroline must keep telling her body to do this until it becomes natural to her!

The pair jump through the combination several times to build their confidence in each other. When Caroline remembers to keep her shoulders back, she jumps all three elements of the coffin more comfortably (pics above).

GETTING TRICKY

Next, Jeanette chooses a trakehner situated off a right-hand turn on level ground. The fence consists of a telegraph pole over a lined ditch. Jeanette advises Caroline to sit up and ride Anna forward round the corner and ride positively toward the middle of the fence. Caroline must also remember to keep looking up (pic right).

Caroline makes a good job of jumping this fence. She sits up and keeps her shoulders back on the approach and is not tempted to look down into the ditch. Caroline has put into practice everything Jeanette has told her and because of this Anna has produced a good jump with no hesitation (pic below).

Trakehner

This type of fence is usually a telegraph pole or log placed on an angle over a ditch. There are various factors which will make this fence more difficult:
- **The approach to the fence**
- **The size of the ditch and whether it is lined or natural**
- **The thickness of the log or rail**

A trakehner is no more difficult than a plain ditch – in fact it can be easier if you can make yourself focus on the rail, not the ditch. Approach in a balanced canter with plenty of impulsion, keep looking ahead and your horse will produce a confident jump.

THE VERDICT

Jeanette is pleased with Caroline and Anna. Caroline took on board everything Jeanette suggested and really tried to put it all into practice. By the end of the lesson they were jumping together much more confidently. Hopefully this will continue to grow and ditches will become easy.

Caroline has found the lesson very interesting and useful. Jeanette highlighted the problems she was having with her position which weren't helping her jumping technique. Caroline now needs to really think about maintaining her new position every time she rides.

Homework

Caroline needs to work on keeping her shoulders back as she approaches the fences and make sure that she allows with her arms so Anna can really use herself over the jump. If Caroline does have any problems she should use her leg, not her hand.

Riding
Advice

Clearly prepared

If your horse jumps well at home but you never manage a clear round at a show, preparation is the key, says Carol Mailer.

You walk the show jumping course with enthusiasm, warm up in the practice arena and then end up being eliminated in your class for three refusals. What has gone wrong and turned your usually willing and obedient horse into an embarrassing and unco-operative nightmare? For many riders the answer is relatively simple: you need to work on your pre-show preparation. This means lots of practice at home, which is the key to solving your problems and gaining success in the arena.

Follow our plan to help iron out any potential hiccups before you get to a show and you'll be in the clear.

HONESTY PAYS

The first step to competing successfully is to be completely honest. Ask yourself whether you and your horse are really ready for the competition. You must be going consistently well over a period of several schooling sessions and be jumping slightly higher and wider than the classes you wish to enter before you think about competing.

It is unfair to expect your horse to jump a bigger track in the ring than he is used to. I am amazed when, after a sticky training session, a client will still declare their intention to compete at the weekend. I point out that they are unlikely to enjoy themselves if they are still at odds with the horse at home and mention that the stress of a show situation is hardly likely to improve their riding or the horse's concentration.

A show is an opportunity to prove how well you have done your homework. So do it. All common disasters can be avoided with some careful preparation.

Carol's tip

■ If your horse changes onto the wrong canter lead, don't be tempted to stop and correct it. This will cause you to lose impulsion and possibly stop at the next fence. Keep riding positively and you will be surprised how well your horse sorts himself out.

REFUSING THE FIRST FENCE

The first fence should be the one to send you confidently on your way round the rest of the track. So why does it so often do the opposite? Mostly, this is due to lack of preparation.

With the best will in the world, your horse will find it difficult to jump an unexpected obstacle easily and his natural reaction will often be to stop in surprise. You know where and what the first fence is, but unless you make it crystal clear to your horse, how can you expect him to read your mind? This is something you must practise at home.

During your training sessions, once you've warmed up, as you begin your approach to the first jump give your horse a clear signal to start. A tap on your knee or your boot with your stick is effective, as long as it isn't too strong to make your horse shoot forward. Sometimes a little touch on the shoulder with a finger is enough to let him know you are ready and he should be too. It doesn't matter what you choose – a good click, an extra nudge with your heel – as long as it lets him know what to expect. This is something you must practise repeatedly at home until it becomes automatic.

If you repeat your own personal signal every time you approach the first fence your horse will be ready. I have lost count of the number of times a disappointed rider tells me that she forgot to signal her horse to start, had a stop at the first fence and then jumped an otherwise immaculate round. It's a totally unnecessary refusal that can so easily be avoided. Just make sure you don't use the stick too enthusiastically. It is meant to be a signal, not a punishment or a threat.

A REFUSAL FURTHER ALONG THE COURSE

The first couple of fences should be encouraging but, as the track turns away from the collecting ring, it's common for a horse to get distracted. If the impulsion is lost, it's not so easy for him to jump and he might stop because of a lack of power. You can develop a positive approach at home. Set your practice fences heading away from home to discover exactly how much extra you need to do to maintain your impulsion and rhythm, and be prepared to do it at a show.

Riding Advice

REFUSAL AT A RELATED DISTANCE

Another problem you might encounter is a double or treble combination that does not suit your horse's stride. Use a tape to measure a variety of distances and set up fences at home. If you pace out the distances without checking them accurately, you may end up jumping your horse over the distances that suit him best, not necessarily the distances you will meet in the ring. Practise working at the distances you know are going to be set in a show jumping class.

If your horse is a little stuffy, work on getting him moving forward more. If he cannot reach the optimum take-off

point, and is too far off the next fence, he has little choice but to stop. Work at home until he consistently produces a more balanced and conventional length of stride. Being too bold or keen, or being ridden too enthusiastically, will give him neither time nor room to come off the floor at the next element. A wise horse will stop rather than land himself in the middle of something and get hurt.

RIDING A CORRECT LINE

Many refusals are caused by the rider not thinking far enough ahead and allowing the horse to land, anticipate the turn, and cut the corner to the next fence. If he cuts the corner, the approach to the next fence will be crabby and cramped. He might not have time to see the fence, and he might lose impulsion by leaning in around the turn and may stop. Your horse is not being naughty – in his brain he knows where he is going so he anticipates the turn. It's up to you to ensure that you hold him out around each turn so he has plenty of room to approach the next jump. This should be a fairly straightforward exercise to do at home as he is bound to know where he is going and will anticipate his route. Practise until you can hold your horse out automatically every time you ride a turn. Only when you can do this every time will you present your horse to his next fence with the best chance of popping it easily.

SPOOKY FILLERS

The problem of unfamiliar jumps is slightly more difficult to remedy at home unless you feel like going mad with a paintbrush.

It is easy for your horse to get into the habit of wanting to examine everything before he leaps. If he has started this aggravating habit, you must set the scene to cure him once and for all, even if it means hiring a course of jumps that will be fresh to him. Many show centres hire out their facilities, and it will be well worth the trip, especially if you can take along someone to help and encourage you.

Make sure the filler you want your horse to jump is small enough to pop from a standstill if necessary. Start with something you are sure he will look at and take care to keep him straight at the middle of the jump. If you allow him to run out the object of the exercise is lost. Stay calm, keep him facing the jump and kick. However sticky he may be, if you nag for long enough he will eventually give way and pop over from a standstill. This is why it's vital to choose a small obstacle. If it is too big your horse might hurt himself and you will do more harm than good.

Don't be tempted to hurry things along with your whip. You don't want your horse to associate a bright new fence with pain. Just prove that you can be more obstinate than him. It simply doesn't work to go faster or ride too sharply with a whip. It might get the horse over one obstacle, but the wrong lesson is learned. Look up as you approach, hold a consistent contact and use lots of leg.

Give your horse only one option – forward and up. He will work out that it is easier and more rewarding to do what you want. Then you will stop nagging him.

Don't keep jumping the same filler once your horse has decided to co-operate. You can't do that in the ring so move straight on to another obstacle. Do exactly the same at the next new filler; again making sure that it is small enough to hop over if necessary. It is vital not to let the horse turn away or duck out. Nag away until you get a result. Jumping over this second filler shouldn't take as long as the first, but stick with it.

By the time you ride your horse at the next filler he should have decided to co-operate. Soon he will adopt a fresh habit of ignoring the appearance of any new fence.

OTHER FACTORS

Everything that happens at a show will either enhance or detract from your horse's performance, you owe it to him to eliminate as many pitfalls as possible. You are trying to cure your horse of stopping, so don't put yourself into a situation which will make things worse:

■ Don't forget the weather. Is your horse perfectly happy to be ridden in a downpour or can he cope with the heat? If you ride in all weathers your horse will probably accept an uncomfortable day as being normal. If you only ever school in ideal conditions, a wet and windy show will come as a bit of a shock.

■ A lack of confidence figures in nearly all incidences of refusals, and slipping on take–off is guaranteed to cause bother. I always recommend using one stud in each shoe, not just in the back shoes, and don't use studs only at shows. Your horse needs to get used to the slightly different but more secure feel when he is wearing them. So don't neglect to put them in at home, even if it is a nuisance.

■ When it comes to equipment, practise riding at home in your competition gear. You don't want any surprises at shows if you find your smart jacket is too tight or your riding boots pinch your feet. Have a proper dress rehearsal with your gear as well as your horse's tack. If you keep your show clothes just for 'best' they will feel unfamiliar and may be enough to detract from the consistency of your riding.

■ If you need to wear spurs at a show, wear them at home too. If you think the horse needs a change of bit or noseband, a show is not the place to try out new equipment.

■ The only surprise your horse should have to cope with on show day is finding himself at a new venue and being expected to perform just as well as he does at home. If everything else is familiar, a trouble–free round should follow.

Hacking for fitness

All riding activities call for **fitness**, from dressage to jumping or distance riding. Whether your **goal** is to compete, to **try something new** with your horse or simply to make the most of the better weather with longer hacks, you'll both **enjoy yourselves a lot more** if your horse is up to the job.

JILL THOMAS is one of Britain's leading endurance riders. A team and individual European gold medallist with Egyptian Khalifa, Jill still holds the British endurance speed record.

Jill's current ride is 15.2hh Arab gelding Tarifya, also known as Max.

When I unloaded Khalifa, the new horse I'd just purchased for the princely sum of £200, everyone was horrified at the bag of bones who shambled across the yard. He didn't look capable of breaking into a trot. But some years later the same horse went on to race over a distance of 102 miles in less than nine hours, setting a European endurance speed record and a British record that still stands.

The incredible fitness Khalifa developed was down to good management and slow, steady training to build strength and stamina. OK, we were training for endurance riding, but the same principles can be applied with great success to any horse.

All riding activities call for fitness, from dressage to jumping or distance riding. Whether your goal this summer is to compete, to try something new with your horse or simply to make the most of the better weather with longer hacks, you'll both enjoy yourselves a lot more if your horse is up to the job. And, with the wintry conditions and short daylight hours finally coming to an end, this is a great time to start planning your horse's fitness programme for the spring and early summer.

You don't need any special facilities or equipment to follow this fitness plan. I've based it on an endurance pattern, which involves plenty of hacking out in the fresh air to improve your horse's physical condition and his mental attitude. We'll be covering all aspects of hacking for fitness, from measuring your horse's progress and making sure he is working effectively to tackling different terrains.

FACTS ABOUT FITNESS

If you've ever reached the top of the stairs puffing and panting with your head pounding, you'll know that being out of shape is no fun. It's simply not fair to expect a horse to work hard without building him up gradually so he becomes accustomed to the extra exertion.

Horses were designed to be on the move constantly, and a fit horse is generally happy and healthy. Watch him turned out in the field and he'll have a natural air of wellbeing and a real interest in life – he'll look as if he feels good about himself.

Not only will your horse find his work more enjoyable if he's in good physical condition, but he'll be able to concentrate more on what you're asking him to do. Being toned and strong puts far less strain on a horse's heart, lungs and legs and greatly reduces the risk of injury. And you'll get fitter as your horse does – an added bonus if you've found that your jods aren't quite as roomy as they used to be.

THE BENEFITS OF HACKING

I've always liked my horses to see the world and learn from being out and about – something essential for the endurance horse but also a real benefit for one competing in any discipline. Coping with natural hazards such as hills, uneven terrain and water certainly teaches a horse to think for himself.

Building a good working relationship with your horse means being on the same wavelength as him. Hacking gives you the time to really get to know one another in a less pressurised environment than an indoor school, allowing you to become familiar with each other's personalities and reactions. Your schooling needn't go out of the window as certain exercises can be practised en route.

A horse who has become stale or dead to the leg after a winter of indoor work will appreciate a change of scenery where the terrain is more challenging. There's lots for him to look at and more for him to think about. He may well become more forward going and develop a keener interest in his work. As well as keeping him on the ball physically, hacking provides a great way to ensure your horse's mind stays sharp and fresh.

From the rider's perspective, an **athletic horse** offers more scope for longer canters and some **exhilarating riding** across varied terrain.

Riding Advice

FIRST THINGS FIRST

Sort out the essentials before you embark upon your fitness programme – you'd be amazed how many people run into problems because they've neglected an area of basic horse management. Ask the vet now if there are any health niggles you're worried about that might interfere with your horse's work.

■ **Feeding**
You may have to re-assess your horse's diet as he takes on more work but don't make any drastic alterations in the early stages

■ **Vaccinations, worming and tooth rasping**
All essential, so make sure everything is in order and up to date.
.
■ **Dust allergies**
An allergy need not prevent your horse from becoming very fit. In fact, his wind, lungs and heart should become stronger and more efficient if he is worked correctly. Ask your vet for advice and devise a method of managing the problem suited to your particular horse.

■ **Feet**
Extra hacking can mean more wear and tear on your horse's hooves, so a conditioning hoof supplement added to his feed will help build stronger horn. An external hoof dressing is also a good idea – I use Keratex twice a week on the hoof wall and sole, applying a diluted solution to the frog.

You don't need special tack to get your horse fit, but ask your farrier whether road studs will help

◼ Shoeing

Discuss your fitness programme with your farrier and ask about road studs if you will be spending more time on slippery surfaces such as tarmac. I prefer to use two small studs in each shoe – one on either side to balance the hoof and avoid any twisting.

THE RIGHT TACK

You won't need any extra equipment as long as your tack fits your horse and is comfortable. The smallest things can irritate your horse over longer distances, so check that numnahs and girth sleeves are without any wrinkles or sharp edges that may rub.

If you use protective boots, take care to wash mud and grit from the inside after every ride. Check that knee boots fit and stay up, otherwise they could become a dangerous hindrance. Safety gear such as lights and reflective clothing is a must.

Don't neglect your own kit. My most important advice is to choose suitable underwear – big knickers may not be very glamorous but they're a whole lot more comfortable than something skimpy!

PLANNING AHEAD

Many riders are hampered in their hacking by the restraints of space and time. I know it can be difficult if there's little land open to you, but don't give up before you've studied a few OS maps for bridleways and contacted your local BHS Bridleways group. It's the only way to become really familiar with what's available in your local area and you may well unearth some overgrown or unknown paths. The Bridleways group can open up a network of opportunities and may also be a good source of hacking partners if you'd rather not ride alone.

If you are limited in off-road riding, approach a local landowner and explain about your training plan. As long as you respect crops and livestock you may well get some support and permission to ride across certain routes or fields.

How about searching your area for country parks or estates? You can buy an annual pass to ride around some of these, and even if they're a trailer-ride away you could team up with friends and their horses for longer trips out at weekends.

Lack of daylight can cause problems if you have little or no access to floodlit facilities, and great caution is necessary on the roads. Until the days get longer the only option may be to ride in your horse's field. There's nothing wrong with this as long as you know the layout and remember any gradients or difficult terrain. If you really want to get your horse fit, set your alarm for an unearthly hour and do the first stages of your training programme in the field. A tip worth remembering is to attach a light to your horse then, if you do part company, you'll be able to locate him in the gloom.

If you're riding alone, don't forget to tell someone where you're going and roughly how long you intend to be. Take your mobile phone if you have one, just in case of emergencies.

If you hack alone, always tell someone where you're going

'During 15 years in the **sport of endurance**, I've taken many horses through the early stages of fitness. Although progress must be **slow and steady**, I always find it rewarding to see my horse develop a sleeker, **more muscular outline** and a beautiful gleaming coat to match.'

Jill Thomas

There are a number of reasons why a particular horse may need a fitness programme. Every horse deserves a holiday once in a while so he can chill out in the field and, while he may not be back to square one in fitness terms, he will need a gradual re-introduction to harder work. Perhaps illness, injury, or a crisis such as last year's foot-and-mouth outbreak has resulted in an enforced lay-off, or maybe the winter with its short daylight hours and unsuitable riding weather has left your horse huffing and puffing at faster paces.

Whatever the reason for his lack of athleticism, the first couple of months in a horse's fitness regime are crucial. It is then that muscle is developed, legs are hardened and the heart and lungs are strengthened for longer, faster work. Any hurrying or cutting corners at this stage can so easily result in injury, so it's well worth taking your time and doing the job properly.

ASSESSING FITNESS

The first step on the road to fitness is to establish your horse's current condition. You'll know from his recent work routine whether he's starting from scratch or already able to cope with a reasonable workload.

A horse who's spent most of the winter in the field with just the odd trip out at the weekend is likely to be in a 'soft' condition, which means he has little strength, stamina or muscle tone. Although some horses keep themselves quite fit in the field, larking about and playing games, you should still start this

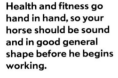

Health and fitness go hand in hand, so your horse should be sound and in good general shape before he begins working.

fittening programme at the beginning.

You may think your horse is fit after a busy winter in the indoor school, but he won't be accustomed to hacking and may find roadwork, longer distances or difficult terrain more of a problem than you imagine. To avoid stresses and strains, take him through the whole programme.

If your horse has been in regular, varied work, compare his daily schedule with the step-by-step guide in this issue and the next one to find out the best point for him to join the programme.

Health and fitness go hand-in-hand, so your horse should be sound and in good

general shape before he begins working. A plump horse will need a bit of slimming down before being asked to do anything too strenuous, while one in poor condition will need building up before his fitness regime can properly begin.

Age is another important consideration. I would not recommend this programme for a horse under six years old, as it is easy to overwork a youngster and cause problems later in life. A horse who's getting on in years will benefit from increased fitness, but be very considerate about his needs and stay alert to any signs that he is not coping.

METABOLIC PARAMETERS

It's handy to know your horse's metabolic parameters at rest – that is his pulse, temperature and respiration rate. Getting a horse fit isn't too scientific, but knowing and monitoring these three things will help you to see how your horse is progressing. They can also be good indicators of illness.

Take the pulse under the jaw or press the base of your palm hard against where the heart is, behind the left elbow. A stethoscope makes this much easier – simply lift the left leg forward and place the stethoscope just in front of where a girth would sit.

The beat should be strong and steady, and between 30 and 44 beats per minute (each beat sounds like a double bump). Take it over a few days to get an accurate average, as the pulse can rise in an instant if the horse is distracted by something. While you are grooming is a good time to try.

A healthy horse's temperature is 38°C (100.4°F), varying no more than half a degree either way.

To calculate your horse's respiration rate, watch his sides as they move in and out with each breath. The resting rate should be around 8-14 breaths per minute.

DEVISING A TRAINING PROGRAMME

I'm always hesitant to offer strict time frames for fitness, as every horse is different and there may be breaks in training or unforeseen problems.

By basing your programme around the following guidelines, you should be in no danger of taking it too quickly. I must stress, however, that this series can only be a guide and the best judge of a horse's ability to train must be his owner.

STEP ONE Walking

30 minutes, increasing to one hour
Half-an-hour of good walking is ample for the first few outings. Aim for an active and engaged walk on a long rein, making sure your horse is swinging along. Just sit quietly, encouraging him if necessary with a schooling whip or a pair of short spurs rather than nagging him every step of the way.

It's much more tiring for the horse if the rider is constantly niggling at his mouth or lurching about with her hands. I was taught to ride carrying two mugs of water, trying not to spill any as I concentrated on keeping my hands steady but soft.

Work your horse for about five days a week, lengthening the duration by 10 minutes or so at a time until you are walking for an hour. This could take around three weeks with a completely unfit horse.

Keep a close eye on how your horse is shaping up. He should be relaxed but interested when out and about, and cool on his return to the yard. Check for rubs, sores, lumps and swellings as you groom him after returning from each ride.

STEP TWO Introducing trot

One hour of walking, building in short periods of trot
The next step is to introduce short periods of trot into your hour of exercise. Stick to a couple of minutes at a time to begin with, building it up gradually.

By week four or five you should be covering six miles within an hour, which equates to an active walk interspersed with a few trots. To calculate the distance, take a piece of thread and an Ordnance Survey map and work out a six-mile route from home using the mileage chart on the map. Then see how long it takes you to complete the route. You'll both get bored if you go the same way every day, so calculate a few different routes with varying terrain.

At this stage you can begin to incorporate some hillwork to build the kind of muscled hindquarters so useful for many horsey sports. Hills are hard work, so walk up to start with. If your horse finds it easier to trot up, allow him to do this and let him walk on a long rein at the top to get his breath.

Tailor your programme to your local terrain. Hilly areas, like my local Cornwall lanes, can really take it out of a horse so you may have to go a bit easier. Similarly, roadwork is more tiring than work on springy ground, so build up the trot very gradually if you're doing a lot on tarmac or a hard, stony surface.

STEP THREE Upping the pace

10 minutes of trotting within the hour, working up to 1¼ hours in total
As you move into week six, build up your trotting to a good 10 minutes within the hour, allowing your horse to move on at an active but collected pace.

If all is going well, increase the length of your hack each outing until you're out for an hour and a quarter, incorporating longer periods of trot. Within that time your horse should be covering eight miles without too much effort.

Get to know your horse and pay particular attention to how he behaves when he returns home. You're aiming for a happy, relaxed attitude, not the look of a horse who's just done a marathon.

WARMING UP AND COOLING DOWN

He may not be doing much activity in the early stages, but your horse still needs to be loosened up before he exerts himself. When you leave the yard, walk actively for a good 10 minutes and always start your trot at a gentle pace.

As horses get fitter, however, they can get fresh and impatient to move up a gear. Rather than having a huge battle or letting him develop an annoying jogging habit, I let Max trot on gently for a few minutes to settle. It gives him more to think about and at least I am asking him to do something rather than saying no all the time.

Arriving back at the yard cool is a must, so walk the last mile home to let your horse wind down.

FITNESS TIPS

1 Try to work as a team with your horse from the start. While it's wrong to accept bad manners, insisting on 100% perfection can soon demoralise a horse. You want him to enjoy his hacking and think for himself rather than behave like a robot.

2 If you have to miss a few days of your programme, simply go back a step when you resume your training. You're asking for trouble if you just press on where you left off.

3 Keep your tack clean as a soft horse is more susceptible to rubs – it's very frustrating to have to halt your training because of a small sore.

4 If you're a bit rusty in the saddle, the programme is a great way to develop your own riding stamina. Remember to do some simple stretches before and after you ride.

5 One way to measure your horse's progress is to take regular photos of him from the side and from behind. Hopefully you'll be amazed at the increasingly athletic animal emerging in front of your eyes as weeks go by!

'As **stress-busters** go there's little to beat tacking up and heading off for a ride through the countryside. For me it's what riding is all about – simply **enjoying the company** of my horse and having the time and space to build a **strong partnership**'

Jill Thomas

I find the hours I spend out training with Max beneficial for both of us. As you and your horse get fitter, you'll develop the confidence to overcome problems together. You'll learn how your horse reacts in different situations and he'll develop the trust to do as you ask him. This bond will prove a real bonus if you're planning to compete in any equestrian discipline this season.

Try using this training programme as a basis to develop as a team with your horse. As an endurance rider I depend on my horse for extreme effort, covering distances of up to 100 miles a day. But at any level of training the aim is to ask your horse rather than tell him, or encourage rather than bully. I don't dictate to Max – in our team, I'm the navigator and he's the pilot.

PROGRESSING YOUR FITNESS PROGRAMME

So far we've looked at how to lay the foundations for fitness. If you've been following this programme your horse should be coping easily with work sessions of around one hour. His legs and respiratory system should be stronger and his overall appearance sleeker and more athletic.

If all the signs are good that your horse is happy with his workload, it's time to push on. Over the next few weeks you can take your horse from a basic level of fitness to a stage where he really is fully muscled and raring to go. You've already done much of the hard work and, as the daylight hours increase and the weather improves, you should find the next few weeks enjoyable and rewarding.

But even the most methodical programme can be interrupted by unexpected health troubles – after all, we're dealing with horses, not machines. It's unlikely that you'll run into problems but, just in case, I've included some troubleshooting tips. Don't panic at a sign of illness or injury. Investigate the problem thoroughly and seek expert advice if you are unsure. Never be tempted to press on with the training regardless, as it does not work.

TAKING THE TRAINING UP A GEAR

If your horse seems to be coping well, you can move on to the next level. By this stage it's impossible to offer any time frames to work to – judge your horse's ability to progress by his appearance, his general attitude and by monitoring the metabolic parameters (pulse, temperature and respiration rate). At this stage you should aim to build up to five or six days' work a week.

STEP FOUR   Introducing canter

Plenty of trot and one or two short canters within a one-and-a-quarter hour outing.
Introduce canter for just a couple of minutes at a time at first, aiming for a springy, controlled pace. Try to remain balanced in the saddle and keep your contact light and steady. Excess movement on your part will only make the job harder for your horse.

STEP FIVE   Longer distances

Building up to one-and-a-half hours.
Increase the canter gradually. You should now be doing longer periods of trot and canter, interspersed with shorter recovery periods at walk. A good day's work will by now consist of a one-and-a half hour ride incorporating all three paces, with your horse moving forwards at around eight-10 miles per hour.

Riding Advice

BUILD YOUR OWN PROGRAMME

The key to success is setting realistic fitness goals for you and your horse and building up gradually.

The fitness plan must work with your lifestyle, so adapt the training into manageable sessions alongside other commitments, such as work and family. Don't become a slave to the programme – it's meant to be fun! No harm will be done if you fancy a lie-in or a weekend away, as long as you lower the intensity a peg or two when you resume training.

Lessons and schooling or lungeing sessions can easily be built into the programme. Just try to work progressively and consistently.

SAMPLE WEEKLY WORKOUT

DAY 1: 1½-hour ride including trot and canter
DAY 2: 1½-hour ride including trot and canter
DAY 3: 1-hour hillwork: just hills, walking up and down
DAY 4: Rest and turnout
DAY 5: 1½-hour ride including trot and canter
DAY 6: Long ride: 2–2½ hours
DAY 7: Rest and turnout

MEASURING PROGRESS

It is possible to take a very technical approach to fitness, but I've based this series on the needs of the average rider rather than the serious endurance competitor.

A simple but effective way to gauge progress is to do exactly the same ride once a fortnight, at the same pace, noting how your horse copes. Take his pulse before you untack him, allowing for any change in climate that might make the ride harder. Then take the pulse again five minutes later. The quicker it falls to his base (resting) rate, the fitter the horse.

Note down whether your horse is coming home fresher and with more energy and watch his general appearance – fitness is evident in a horse with a healthy bloom to his coat and a bright, alert attitude.

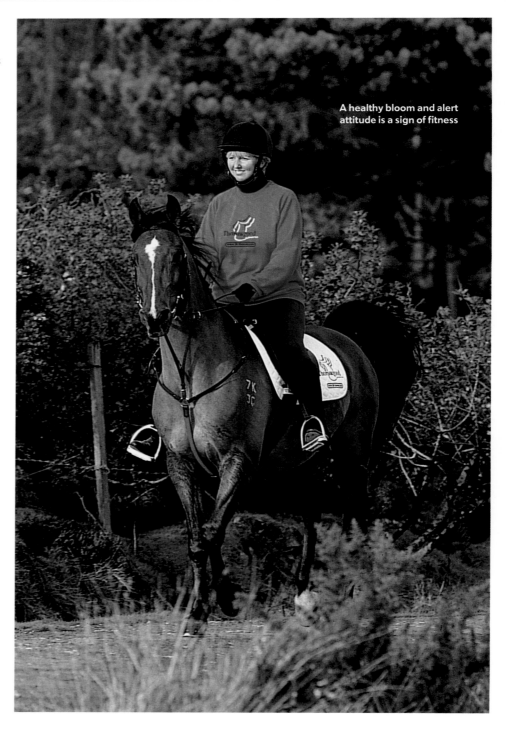

A healthy bloom and alert attitude is a sign of fitness

TROUBLESHOOTING

Behaviour

Rushing home: Clever thinking is called for here. Before he gets too fit and becomes a real handful, work out zigzagging routes so your horse never learns to recognise the point at which he turns back towards his stable. Incorporate half-halts and halts into your outings to keep your horse working and his brain occupied. At various points along the ride ask him to stand for just a few seconds, make a big fuss of him and gradually increase the length of the halts as he learns to wait calmly.

Laziness or napping: A horse can nap, or refuse to go forward, for a number of reasons. Napping can vary in degrees from mild reluctance to full-blown refusal to go anywhere.

First, rule out any physical reasons and re-assess your horse's diet and stable routine. Check that your tack fits well and does not rub or pinch. Are you light with your hands, or is the horse scared of going forwards into the bridle? A lesson with a good instructor may help solve the problem.

Take a positive approach and use a schooling whip and a pair of short spurs to back up your leg aids if necessary. Riding out with a forward going companion can help, but try to stay beside the other horse rather than getting a tow behind him. Ask the other rider to slow down gradually so you can work side by side or take the lead occasionally.

Progress may be slow, but persevere as the end result will be a horse you can enjoy.

Health

Lameness: Typical causes include bruised soles or corns, both of which your farrier can help sort out. Windgalls can occur with increased work but the effects are usually just cosmetic. You may know when the lameness occurred, if your horse steps on a stone for example, or perhaps your horse has a minor lameness that clears up with cold hosing and rest. Ask your vet about anything more persistent that may be worrying you.

Overtraining: We all have off days and a horse is the same. If he has become a little jaded with the workload he may benefit from a mini holiday of a couple of days of turnout. If he's still lethargic or disinterested, reassess his training and diet

Let your horse drink when out on a ride

and perhaps add a feed supplement – phone a nutritionist for expert advice. Consult your vet if your horse fails to perk up after a short break.

Tack

Saddle fit: Your horse will be muscling up and changing shape, so check the fit of your saddle regularly. You may need to call in the saddler for a professional assessment.

Bitting: A horse with a sore mouth needs rest and perhaps a different bitting arrangement. Take a look at your riding technique too, and have a few flatwork lessons if necessary to sort out any braking problems.

Rubbing: Tack that you thought fitted well may start to irritate or rub your horse over longer distances. Keep all saddlery and accessories clean and supple, and use easy-care products where possible.

Tackling longer distances

Warming up and cooling down: Set off for each ride in walk to let your horse loosen up, or at a gentle trot if he is keen to get going. It's really important to walk for long enough (say a mile) at the end of the ride to allow your horse to arrive back at the yard cool and relaxed.

At this stage of the training programme, it will benefit your horse to give him as much time out in the field as you can.

Drinking: While we're out I let Max drink as much and as often as he wants. Many people are surprised to hear this, but there's more danger in denying a horse water and then letting him gulp down a full bucket when he gets home. If your horse drinks from a cold stream, go steady for a few minutes to allow the water in his gut to warm up. You can move off more quickly if he has been drinking from a warm puddle.

Boredom: Avoid the onset of any behavioural problems by varying the route and the direction you go in, and riding out both alone and in company.

Ask your farrier for help with bruised soles or corns

Choose tack that's comfortable and fits well

Riding Advice

Photography: **David Miller**

'Learning to cope with the demands of **the great outdoors** will give your horse a mental workout as well as a **physical challenge**. With a little extra training he could soon become a real all-terrain animal'

Jill Thomas

The real benefit of hacking for fitness is that broadening your horse's mind through a diverse work schedule should really help in all aspects of your horse's life. He'll be more relaxed in his stable, calmer at shows and events, and more willing to try new activities such as gridwork sessions or cross-country jumping. Of course, he could gain a degree of physical stamina simply by cantering in circles in the school, but where would you rather be?

If you've been following my fitness plan, as well as developing stronger legs and more energy, your horse will have been gaining confidence in coping with hacking hazards. To the novice or young horse the outside world can be a scary place but, with time, your horse will learn to deal with varied terrain and strange situations.

Certain hacking situations may also be new to the rider. Learning how to guide your horse across boggy going or through water will help you develop your riding skills and gain confidence in your abilities.

Just as we've stepped up the work rate over the weeks, you must expand your horse's mind in gradual stages. Plunging straight into sticky situations may frighten your horse or result in an injury, so take it steady with new experiences until you both feel happy to move on.

Top tip

■ If you're riding on a track that becomes wet or boggy, try to follow previous hoofprints across the firmer parts. If this is not possible, slow right down and stay to the side where the mud should be shallower. Let the horse lower his head to see where he's going but don't drop the rein contact completely.

Encourage the horse to work it out for himself by sitting still and asking him gently but firmly with your legs. Don't bully him through – gain his trust so he'll go forwards without panicking. If you get in a flap he may well leap through and lose a shoe or frighten himself.

TERRAIN TRAINING

To fully explore the countryside, you need a horse capable of covering different conditions underfoot.

Roadwise

Ride according to the state of the road. You can move forwards at an active trot on level tarmac, but beware of working too fast or too hard and causing concussion. Ask your farrier to fit a set of road studs if you need extra grip and choose the roughest part of the road, usually the edge or the middle (depending on traffic conditions). On very steep or slippery tarmac it may be necessary to dismount and lead your horse.

Contact the British Horse Society for more information about riding safely on the roads and seek expert advice if your horse lacks confidence in traffic. Busy roads are no place to take risks.

Over stones

As an experienced endurance horse, Max has been trained to pick his way at speed across rough tracks and boulder-strewn paths. Don't avoid stones – let your horse find his way across, slowly at first then with a bit more gusto. If he has good feet you can pick up speed as he becomes more sure-footed.

Some people fit pads between the hoof and the shoe to cushion the sole, but I'm not keen on this idea. I've found that the silicone needed under each pad can soften the sole and that the cushioning effect of the pad can move the nails and loosen the shoe. Hoof pads are necessary for some horses, but I prefer to first try hardening the feet over a period of time with regular applications of a hoof dressing such as Keratex.

On the beach

Firm sand is a great surface to work on, but watch out for shingle or soft patches that can pull a tendon. Unless you know the beach, first walk the route to check for good going. Then you know it's safe to ride back at a faster speed over your horse's hoofprints. The best place to ride is at the waterline in a couple of inches of lapping water, as this reduces concussion during fast work. You're likely to get very wet, but then that's half the fun!

WATER

Few horses are natural water-lovers, so plenty of patience is needed to produce one who tackles the stuff with confidence. Kindness and repetition will help your horse overcome any fears he has.

First steps

Try to think as your horse does. If he's faced with a stretch of water, he doesn't know how deep it is or what lurks under the surface. To go through it he must put his trust in you, so the key is to start slow and progress steadily. After all, your horse will remember his early experiences for the rest of his life.

Start with a shallow patch of still water with an inviting entrance and firm ground underfoot. I prefer to lead the horse through at first, so I wear gloves, waterproof boots and a riding hat and take the reins over his head for more control.

Approach the water and allow your horse to lower his head to sniff and stare. He'll develop more courage if he makes the decision to move forwards himself, so splash about in the water yourself if necessary and encourage him to come to you. Just be prepared for a sudden leap if he decides to take the plunge.

Any signs of progress should be rewarded with loads of praise and reassurance. There's no rush – keep the outings short and don't push too hard. As long as he's had a go, your horse should be made a big fuss of and taken away until the next time.

On board

Repeat the same procedure while on the horse, letting him lower his head and look before putting a bit of pressure on him to encourage him to pick his way through. Before long he should be happy to walk through or stand in the water.

As he develops confidence you can ask him to try crossing deeper water and running streams, but don't be tempted to undo all your hard work by asking too much too soon. Always be prepared to backtrack to something easier if necessary.

In deeper

An endurance horse may have to go through moving water up to chest deep. Max wasn't a big fan of water, so I've had to work to gain his trust. Even so, he still skirts round the odd murky puddle if given the choice.

Frustrating as this may be, I never make it into a big issue. A good working relationship involves a bit of give and take – plus there could be sharp stones at the bottom of the puddle that could cause an injury.

HACKING HAZARDS

Whether it's a plastic fertilizer sack flapping in a hedge or a tractor reversing into a gateway, there's plenty going on out there to give an unsuspecting horse a fright. But, with the right approach, you can accustom him to take almost anything in his stride.

Putting yourself in your horse's shoes for a moment can help you to understand his way of thinking. He doesn't know exactly what the strange obstacle is and, without any means of defence at his disposal, his first reaction is to flee. With a combination of good schooling and some confidence on your part, he'll learn that there's nothing to worry about and that staying calm is his best strategy.

Tackle a spooky obstacle quietly and slowly, using firm but kind persuasion to encourage your horse past. Don't turn his head towards it and force him to confront the monster. Make a real fuss of your horse as he passes it, even if he does seem to grow extra legs and crawl by like a deranged spider!

Depending upon the location, it may be safe to allow your horse to have a proper look at the obstacle. Ideally, take the time to let him gain the courage to go up and sniff it. Jump off and stand by, or sit on, the thing yourself if you can to show him just how friendly it really is.

Do your homework

Familiarise your horse with as much as you can at home. Tie a plastic bag high up in the field hedge, out of reach, but near enough to him so he becomes accustomed to it over time. Cover some of the ground by the field gate with plastic so he gets used to walking near it and, eventually, over it. Encourage your horse to remain quiet and calm as he learns to deal with these hazards.

Bad manners

In some cases a horse may develop a habit of shying or spooking out of sheer naughtiness or high spirits. Remind your horse of his manners if you suspect he's simply trying it on, and maybe book a lesson or two for some expert help in keeping any disobedience in check. Incorporating schooling exercises such as leg-yielding and half-halts into your hacking will keep your horse's brain occupied and discourage him from any mischief.

While it's important that your horse behaves himself out hacking, try not to be too oppressive by demanding 100% perfection all of the time. Give him the benefit of the doubt if he does find something scary and always be quick with plenty of words of praise.

To fully explore **the countryside**, you need a horse capable of covering **different conditions** underfoot.

Tackle spooky objects quietly and slowly

Mirror image

**The way your horse goes is a direct reflection of your riding, says Joni Bentley.
Improve your position and balance and the result will be mirrored in your horse.**

Most riders acknowledge that their mental state, position, balance and weight distribution greatly influence their horses' way of going. This, in turn, affects his behaviour and therefore his potential. However, not many people seem to consider the true implications of this fact. This knowledge led me to ask whether our unsoundness as riders could be affecting our horses' soundness. Excluding horses who have suffered previous accidents or congenital disorders, I think the answer is yes. I strongly believe that the root cause of many horses' unsoundness is their riders' positional problems.

If horse and rider do not work in unity, instead of being a flowing and elegant whole, they become two entities at odds with each other. Although they try to go in the same direction, they pull in different ones, fighting each other's movement.
My experience as an Alexander teacher and horse trainer has shown me how much one side of the partnership depends on the accuracy and skill of the other. When both sides work together, the results can be fantastic.

'I strongly believe that the **root cause** of many horses' unsoundness is their **riders' positional** problems.'

Joni Bentley developed the Bentley Technique in 1994 and she now travels internationally running Bentley Technique courses and teaching riders of all ages and levels. Joni qualified as an Alexander Technique teacher (a three-year course) in 1993 and has been a qualified riding teacher since 1984.

THE IMPORTANCE OF POSITION

The position of the rider is one of the most basic aspects of riding. However, it seems to me that it is often forgotten in conventional training where so much emphasis is put on the horse.

The optimum rider position is relaxed and free from tension and does not hinder the horse in any way. It allows him optimum use of his body. When the rider is in this relaxed state, she no longer subconsciously fights the movement of the horse, grips with the reins, or hinders the horse.

As an Alexander teacher, I know that most of us do not conform to ideals but I believe problems often occur when instructors try to force tense riders into an ideal position that their normally sedentary bodies simply can't manage.

SITTING TO ONE SIDE

Another common problem I see is riders sitting to one side.

That might not sound like a big deal but such imbalance can cause grievous damage to the horse. The rider's uneven weight distribution makes it impossible for the horse to relax and work equally on both reins. Sitting slightly to one side not only places pressure on the horse's ribs, interfering with his co-ordination, balance and muscular development, it also places more pressure down one side of the horse's legs, damaging both bone and soft tissue.

Commonly riders sit too far to the right, as a result of being right handed. The right side of their body is stronger, but also stiffer because it is more compressed and shortened. This extra strength pulls the rider over that side of the horse.

This is the same rider viewed from behind. You can see that she is sitting to the right and her right stirrup is longer.

THE IMPLICATIONS FOR THE HORSE

A rider with no strength in her position will have no influence over the horse's quarters and he will therefore have no impulsion. A horse working without impulsion will be unable to engage his quarters and lighten his forehand.

Many riders arriving at my workshops have hollow backs and trailing quarters, through trying to force themselves into an upright seat as required by their trainer who tells them to sit up straight. Many of them complain of lower back pain.

In this position the rider's weight is more concentrated at the base of the pommel. This affects the reflex point at the base of the horse's wither which stimulates him to drop his back and trail his quarters.

Here you can see the effects on her horse. Rather than tracking his left hindfoot forwards and up into the track of his left forefoot, he crosses it sideways and under. This pushes horse and rider sideways and the crookedness is reflected in the horse's head and neck. This faulty action is common and is the reason so many riders struggle to get impulsion, energy and elevation.

Below: Under-using one side of the body puts strain on the other. You can see the outward twist of the horse's right haunch starting at the pelvis, through the stifle, hip and fetlock – his right hock appears to be bowing outwards. This is a typical biomechanical problem.

Left: Carol suffers from backache and tells me that for years she has been shouted at to sit up straight and put her shoulders back.

Above: A hollow rider puts more weight on her pubic bone which presses down into the base of the pommel, causing the horse to drop his back and rush forward, pulling the rider off her seat. This has caused Carol's seat to shoot to the back of the cantle.

Left: After some dismounted Alexander work, we achieve a sound biomechanical upright position.

Above: When this is transferred to the horse, you can see he responds beautifully. We have loosened the rein to show he is rounding up into self-carriage without force.

Biomechanics Biomechanics is the mechanics of movement of living creatures. The body is naturally designed to work in a biomechanically sound way. We interfere with this natural movement by pulling and pushing it to fit what we think is the ideal image.

In this photo you can see Carol is falling in. This action knocks the horse off balance. As he falls in, he uses his head and neck to rebalance. He also drops his back and trails his quarters, leaving his back unsupported and vulnerable to wear and tear. It is pointless trying to fix the horse's head down (as so many do) at this stage when it is the rider who needs the adjustment.

I ask Carol to examine how her seat is absorbing the horse's movement by placing a hand under her seat to see if one seatbone is further back than the other. She immediately notices how her left seat bone is tighter and further back than her right. If one hip is stiffer than the other it can prevent the horse from lifting up his back on that side and the stiffness will transfer to the horse causing him to take a shorter step on that side. I see many riders blocking their horses in this way. Unfortunately, the ultimate consequence is an unlevel action.

WHEN RIGHT FEELS WRONG

Without the correct training the problem is difficult to cure because, to right-handed riders, this position feels more familiar and safe. When asked to sit more over to the left (ie centrally) they are reluctant to leave their familiar safety zone. When I guide a rider who has been sitting habitually to the right into straightness, she is convinced I am crazy. The resistance in her mind fights the new sensations because it feels awkward, different and wrong.

To illustrate my point, lace your fingers together and then undo them about five times. As you do so, notice which thumb lies on top.

Now repeat the exercise, consciously organising your fingers and thumbs in a way that the other thumb lands on top. Does it feel right or wrong? Then do the same exercise folding your arms and crossing your legs.

SEEING IS BELIEVING

Well aware of this faulty sensory appreciation (and to stop me going crazy), the Bentley Technique training starts on a wooden horse in front of a web cam. This enables pupils to see if what they are doing is what they think they are doing.

When working on the saddle horse, students are mesmerised to see themselves from different angles on the computer screen. They recognise that their right stirrup is about 4" lower than the left and that when they stand evenly over the left and right stirrups, they feel as though they are falling way off to the left. For the first time, students acknowledge that their aids to the horse are confusing. They usually respond by asking: "Why have my past instructors not pointed out my lopsidedness to me?"

I use corrective dismounted work to straighten Carol's pelvis and mobilise her hips. Mounted again, she is amazed at how much more active and free her left seat bone is. Unhindered by her blocking seat bone, the horse lifts his back and uses his left haunch correctly and with power.

CASE STUDY

My student Irene Ridler has owned Charley for many years. He had always suffered from a problematic bone spavin in his right hindleg which required bute. After Bentley Technique lessons Irene is now reaping the reward of sorting out her position. "Charley is now moving more freely than ever before. In the past, he used to develop stiffness after standing still, even for a short while. He now moves off freely and easily."

As well as the financial benefits of not having to spend money on unnecessary medicines, Irene also has the knowledge that her riding is not inflicting damage on her horse and she has improved her dressage marks. Irene is upset that Charley's condition was explained away as 'just one of those things'. Interestingly, the two horses she had before Charley also had bone spavin on the same hindleg!

Going straight

Get your hips supple and mobile and your horse's movement will be straight and free, says Joni Bentley.

When you have successfully mastered these exercises, your horse will begin to stretch his spine and lower his neck because you have released your stiff side.

To illustrate this point perfectly, try this exercise with a friend. Take turns to play the part of horse and rider. I promise, the results will amaze you.

The suppleness and straightness of the rider's hips affect the way the horse's hindquarters develop and function. For a horse to advance in his training without breaking down, he must use the correct postural muscles and the rider must be straight and able to fully absorb his movement.

In order for the horse to work well with impulsion and lightness, he must step well under his body with his hindlegs. To do this he needs to be able to lift the rider's seat bone forward and up as he lifts each hindleg, carrying his rider's weight effortlessly.

In my opinion, if one of the rider's seat bones is locked or not supple, it blocks the horse's movement. He responds the only way he can by taking a short step. If the rider has one stiff hip, the horse will develop an unlevel action on the same side. This is often called bridle lameness, but I call it rider lameness. Eventually the horse, like the rider, begins to suffer from lower back problems.

MOUNTED EXERCISE

Ask a friend to work with you during this exercise to be your eyes on the ground and give you feedback.

Ask them to stand behind you and check that you are sitting straight as you walk away from them by watching the horse's dorsal line. When it drops to the left, your left side and hip should drop to the left. When the dorsal line drops to the right, your pelvis should do the same.

In the beginning, you will probably find that you drop further to 3 o'clock than you do to 9 o'clock. Because most of us are one sided, our spines are stiff one way, but a deep, absorbing seat is equal on both sides. This lopsidedness robs you of the full use of your left leg, so use the exercises on the page to straighten up.

EXERCISE TO INCREASE FEEL

Sit in the saddle on the lowest part of your seat bones, balanced between the ball and heel of your seat feet. As your horse steps under with his inside hindleg, try to notice whether you are allowing him to lift your inside seat bone forward and up. When you feel your inside seat bone being lifted say "now" out loud. Ask your friend to check your timing is correct.

Now work on your outside seat bone. Ask your friend to walk behind you and say "now" as your horse drops your outside seatbone. Ask your friend to keep calling until you can feel the movement for yourself. When you're confident, say "now" out loud and ask your friend to check you timing.

The following exercises will give you an insight into your own crookedness and tension and show you where you may be blocking your horse. Practising these exercises regularly will help you:
- Become more supple and straight
- Be more able to engage your horse's (and your own) quarters
- Enjoy your horse's improved way of going
- Achieve riding success without stress

Mobilising the pelvis with the pelvic clock

1 Draw a clock face on an A3 piece of paper, place it on a chair or saddle horse and sit on it in front of a mirror. Make sure 12 o'clock is in front of you, 6 o'clock is behind you, 3 o'clock is to your right and 9 o'clock is to your left. You can also try these exercises mounted, either while being led or on the lunge.

2 Place your hands underneath your seat bones, palms facing upwards and find the lowest part. Even up the weight on your left and right seat bones. Remove your hands and imagine that your seat bones are little feet, the front of your seat bone is the ball of the foot, the back is the heel.

3 Rock your pelvis towards 12 o'clock (see pic right) so that you rest on the ball of your seat feet. See how far onto the ball you can move. Come back to the centre and repeat the exercise a few times, taking it slowly and easily.

4 Now rock your pelvis back towards 6 o'clock so that you rest more on the heel of your seat feet. See how far back you can take your pelvis without falling backwards. Come back to centre and repeat a few times. I find most riders have a hollow lower back until, like our horses, they are trained to bring their quarters underneath themselves. If you find it easier to move to 12 than 6 o'clock, place your legs over the front flap of the saddle and move your seat bones further forward and under you (see pic right).

5 Bring your legs back into riding position very slowly. Move one leg a tiny amount then the other. Stop if there is a hint that you are tipping towards 12 o'clock and wait for any tightness to stretch and release. Watch yourself in the mirror and work on this until you can move as far backwards (towards 6 o'clock) as you can forwards (towards 12 o'clock). Then you can progress to the next exercise.

6 Lean your pelvis sideways down to 3 o'clock rocking onto the outer edge of your right seat foot and the inner edge of your left seat foot. Watch that you do not hollow your back or twist.

7 Come back to the centre and go to 9 o'clock (pic right). Many students struggle with this part of the clock because they naturally sit to the right. They evade by pushing the right side of the pelvis forward while leaning into the left groin. This is the reason so many horse and rider partnerships tip in on the left rein. To work through this, use your abdominal muscles to push down to 6 o'clock, then move to 7, 8 and 9 o'clock but don't allow the right side of your pelvis to push forwards and lead the movement.

8 Now start to move around the clock. Start at 12 o'clock and rotate your pelvis to 1 o'clock, come back to 12 o'clock and then return to centre. Then start at 12 o'clock and work your way around to 2 o'clock, work back to 12 o'clock and back to the centre. Continue with this exercise until you have gone the whole circumference of the clock in both directions. Work on the direction or areas of the clock face that are more difficult for you.

Hitting the right note

Riding to music is a great way to regulate your horse's paces and improve your rhythm as a rider. It's also becoming a popular competition discipline. Jo Sharples explains how to tune in to the benefits.

"There's no question in my mind **that music** helps the rider maintain rhythm. It's like **dancing** with somebody – perhaps one of you is the slightly dominant partner, but you both adjust to **each other's rhythm**."

G o into any gym or aerobics class and you'll see that music is an essential part of the human workout. It's been shown to act as a powerful motivator, as well as regulating speed, rhythm and effort.

So why not ride to music for much the same reasons? Dressage to music competitions are increasing in popularity and have proved to be a big pull for spectators. Even if you are not interested in competing, there are still plenty of good reasons to get your horse dancing.

"I'm a firm believer in the value of riding to music, we have a sound system in the school which plays all day," says Olympic dressage rider Richard Davison. "It has revolutionised the popularity of dressage as a competitive sport, but it's also a great mood enhancer to use at home.

"There's no question in my mind that music helps the rider maintain rhythm. It's like dancing with somebody – perhaps one of you is

the slightly dominant partner, but you both adjust to each other's rhythm."

Which is why you should think beyond using music just to help your flatwork, says accredited event trainer and FEI International Event Judge, Les Smith.

"Schooling to music is useful whether it's over poles and fences or on the flat," he says. "The key to good jumping is rhythm. If you imagine a jump as an extended canter stride, you can see how helpful it might be to work to music. It can be particularly beneficial for tense riders or nervous horses too, provided you choose something calming or soothing."

In fact, the only off-putting fact about riding to music is the length of time it can take to find the right material for your horse. However, even this can be a fun and worthwhile exercise if you think of it as investing time in getting to know your horse's rhythm, tempo, stride length and speed at all paces.

If you're distracted or hassled, you have to get rid of that before you get on a horse, and the right music can help you focus on your schooling. I use Bon Jovi to psyche myself up for big competitions too!

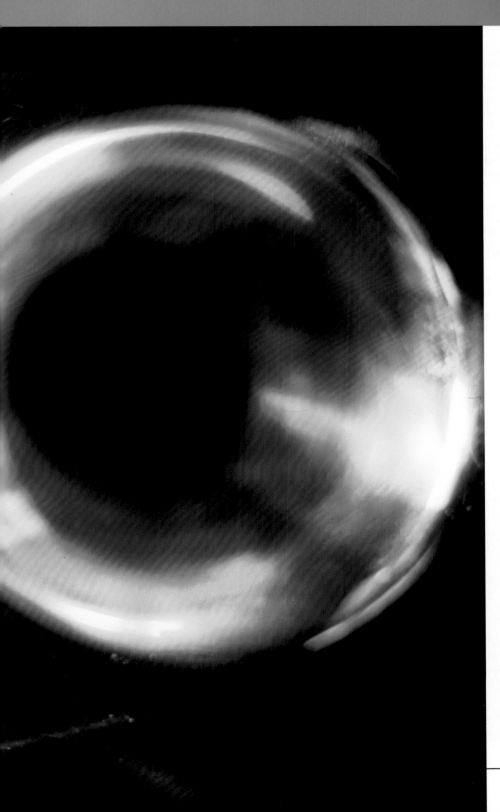

How to start

CHOOSING MUSIC

"Try to sum up your horse's character. Most owners can imagine exactly what type of music he would choose to listen to if he was human," says dressage to music specialist Claire Moir, who puts together routines for many of the dressage elite as well as competing at Prix St Georges level. "Airy fairy ballet music might not suit a heavy cob, for example. The music also has to match the horse's paces and allow for changes of pace and rhythm. Don't just go for your own particular favourites – listen to the radio and borrow music from friends until you find something which really fits in with your horse. Try to find things other people haven't already used, as there's nothing worse for the judge and spectators than hearing the same old things," she advises.

It's unlikely that one piece of music will fulfil all your requirements, so you need to copy chunks of the pieces which you feel suit your horse best from record, tape or CD. Editing and mixing music into a suitable routine of the required length is time consuming, but don't be put off. You don't have to be gifted musically to do it successfully, you just need to hear the rhythm and beat which fit in with your horse's paces.

Keep it simple to start with and stick to one piece of suitable music per pace ie walk, trot and canter. Later, you can add to your horse's repertoire and build up a bigger selection. Aim for smooth changes with no gaps between different pieces by keeping the volume identical and preferably staying with the same style or tone of music – unless you're aiming to shock!

Be safety conscious and if you need an extension lead, use one designed for outdoor use. A battery-operated stereo or even a car radio at full blast will also do the job. A personal stereo will help you stay rhythmic, but why cut the horse out of the equation? However, it can be useful when you are experimenting with different music or learning a new routine where you may need to keep changing and replaying the music.

If your aim is to compete, bear in mind that tests are judged 50% on technical performance (accurate and correct movements, rhythm, energy, elasticity and harmony between horse and rider) and 50% on artistic merit (which includes freedom and regularity of paces, impulsion, lightness, suitable choice and interpretation of music and choreography). So choice of music really will affect your final result.

PUTTING TOGETHER A ROUTINE

Guesswork will rarely give a slick result. The following are useful aids:

1 A stopwatch to count the number of steps per minute at each pace (Count the steps for fifteen seconds and multiply by four. Do it several times to get a good average)

2 A metronome to work out the speed and rhythm of each pace, which you can then set up at home with music on hand

3 A video of your horse working at all paces and performing various movements, or an entire test, which you can study with the music at home

"I often just use background music when at home because the horses find it soothing, but if you're competing, then you need to be very precise. You'll also need someone with a stopwatch or video to help you," says Claire. "Work out your routine first, incorporating the required movements and videoing the whole lot, then fit it to suitable music. To keep it simple first time round, try writing the test in three blocks of walk, trot and canter, which you can time and fit to three blocks of suitable music. Then simply repeat it on the other rein. That way, the judge knows where you're going, it doesn't look too bitty and the margins for error are reduced.

"Alternatively, you can try to make the movements fit into your chosen music programme by timing each musical phrase and matching them to particular movements required in the test. Make sure you leave some breathing spaces at key points throughout the test, such as before an important transition, so you can give yourself time to get to the right place in the arena to match the music."

There are freestyle to music classes at all levels from riding club to national championships, Novice to Grand Prix. Each has a time limit and a number of compulsory movements to be included. Copies are available from British Dressage. For example, novice requirements include a 15m circle in trot, a 20m circle in canter, lengthened strides at trot, at least 20m medium walk and free walk on a long rein. Elementary asks for collected trot, shoulder in and counter canter. The time limit is between four and four-and-a-half minutes, taken from the first halt to the final salute. Points are deducted for time faults and for including movements not normally performed at that level.

You do not have to use the markers in a music test, but they may help you with the accuracy and structure of your routine. Use the whole arena and try to work equally on each rein.

You will have to adjust and ride through the piece several times before you are happy, but don't skimp on this or try to force something to work – it's better to have a routine which doesn't push the horse out of his natural rhythm.

Be familiar with your test and ride it through a few times

THE LEGALITIES

It is illegal to reproduce music in a public performance without permission. British Dressage holds a licence, which covers affiliated shows, and an agreement also exists with British Riding Clubs. Unaffiliated shows are not covered, unless by separate arrangement. Ignorance is no defence and infringement of copyright can be a serious and expensive business. If you are in any doubt, check that the show organiser has the relevant licence. You could also confirm with the following:

1 The Licensing Department at the Performing Rights Society grants licences on behalf of the composers and publishers of the music. These are usually granted to the organiser or venue. Contact: PRS Ltd, 29-33 Berners St, London W1P 4AA

2 Phonographic Performances Ltd grants licences to organisers or venues to allow recorded music to be played in public. Contact: PPL, Ganton House, 14-22 Ganton St, London W1V 1LB

3 You may need a Limited Availability Licence from the Mechanical Copyright Protection Society to re-record music (for example to copy a CD onto tape). The price depends on how much music you tape and how many copies you make. Contact: MCPS Ltd, 41 Streatham High Road, London SW16 1ER.

For more information or copies of rules and requirements, contact British Dressage at the NAC, Stoneleigh, Kenilworth, Warks CV8 2RJ. Tel: 02476 698830

Top tips
- Buy good quality blank tapes even if they are a little more expensive
- Get together with friends and practise as a quadrille – it's fun and a great way to sharpen up your precision, control and concentration
- If you are preparing for a display rather than competition, design your routine around where the audience is located
- Think ringcraft – ride your more advanced movements coming towards the judge, and design your test to help yourself and the horse.
- Dig out old test reports and note the judges' comments and marks for different movements, then play to your horse's strengths
- Different surfaces can affect your timing and rhythm. Being thoroughly familiar with your test can help you deal with this
- You will make life difficult for yourself if your test is totally dependent on perfect rhythm and timing, so don't select music with a very dominant beat until you are sure your horse will maintain the rhythm, even away from home

Stirrup contact

Achieving perfect balance between your stirrups in rising trot will help your horse find his natural rhythm and grace, says Joni Bentley.

The correct trot rhythm for each individual horse is his personal, unique signature. I think it's one of the most exciting things to find. In well-bred unspoiled horses, the rhythm naturally expresses itself in harmony and elevation. I believe many horses never find their true signature because their rider restricts their potential. A rider who is not balanced or has a hollow back, blocks the horse's natural rhythm and causes him to push off stiffly with his hindlegs out behind him, forcing him onto his forehand.

CORRECTING A HOLLOW BACK
Exercise 1
The only way to truly correct a hollow lower back is to deepen your leg position. Do this in rising trot and hold the pommel during this exercise. As you rise, push your knee back in such a way that you feel a deep stretch all the way down the back of your leg. Stretch your calf muscle and allow your heel bone to sink deeper. Finish by relaxing the front of your ankles, backs of your knees, and the front of your hips.

ACHIEVING LATERAL BALANCE
Exercise 2
Now you are straight in profile, it's time to check your lateral balance. Do this exercise mounted at halt and ask a friend to stand behind you and give you feedback. Stand up in your stirrups and imagine your feet are standing on a clock face between 3 o'clock and 9 o'clock.

Keep your body vertical and try to step with your left leg to 9 o'clock. It should feel as if you are lifting your leg away from the saddle and the horse's side. It should appear to your friend that the left stirrup is slightly lower than the right. Don't allow your body to lean to the left, just try to move your leg. It should not feel as if you are dragging the saddle across to one side. Return to your normal position and then step to 3 o'clock. Now the right stirrup should be slightly lower.

Ask your friend to confirm you are doing this correctly. Work with your friend's feedback until you can step equally to the left and right on your horse, and then balance between the two with a 50:50 contact in each stirrup.

Once you have achieved this, go into rising trot and notice whether the contact remains even. Ask your friend for feedback. While performing this exercise, even if you cannot feel it, your friend on the ground will see how your whole body naturally organises itself above your feet.

stirrup contact while riding.

Your stirrups are your main point of contact during rising trot, so use them to test your straightness by assessing how much weight you have in each one at any time. Work towards maintaining a 50:50 balance in your stirrups at all times when riding.

In the photo left, you can see that Carol has hardly any weight in her left stirrup, it's all over to the right. She needs to even up her stirrup contact in order to bring herself and her horse back into balance.

It always seems strange to me that, although there is so much talk about rein contact, there is little mention of stirrup contact. With more attention focused here, I feel there would be far fewer horses suffering from strains and back pain.

After reading this feature, look around you and I'm sure you will see riders and horses tipping around corners. Using these Bentley Technique exercises will ensure you remain straight and upright while riding on a straight line and around corners and circles.

THIGHS AND LEGS
Exercise 3

Now your stirrup contact is developed and you are rising equally with a 50:50 contact in each stirrup, we can add the next stage. In halt, stand up in the stirrups and ask your friend to place her hand on the inside front of your thigh. Your helper should keep her hand still as you sit and rise, as if trotting. As you rise make sure the front of your thigh rolls into her hand. Ask her to tell you when she feels a firm pressure against her hand.

When this is established all the way down the thigh to the knee on both legs, practise the exercise in walk. Check your stirrup contact is even throughout.

LOWER LEG
Exercise 4

Now work on the lower legs and feet. Practise in halt first. Rise as if you were trotting and make little inward circles with your toes, pointing them towards the horse. You will feel as though you are pigeon toed. This exercise flexes and supples your ankle joints, while keeping the inside of your calf on the horse. Get a helper to assist your rotations if necessary. With this established, ask your horse to stretch his neck down by gently massaging his ribcage with your calves.

Once you have perfected these exercises in halt, it's time to develop your

BALANCED TROT
Exercise 5

It's easiest to do this exercise on the lunge. Go on the right rein and repeat Exercise 2, this time in trot. Ask your friend to watch you and check that your left stirrup is slightly lower than your right as you step to the left. This time, as you stand to the left, allow your spine to bend to the right and absorb the movement of your leg. It should feel as is there is a kink in your spine.

When you have mastered 9 o'clock, work on 3 o'clock. This time, as you rise, allow your spine to bend to the left as your body accommodates the new leg position. You will probably find that you are very stiff on one side (usually to 9 o'clock), and this is the side you should work on. Riding in this way will ensure that your spine and hips stay supple and you will become equal on both reins, fully absorbing the horse's movement. Only then will your horse find his true signature.

A WORD OF WARNING

If your saddle is too narrow at the pommel, it will pinch or rub your horse's wither when you stand in your stirrups, and this can cause muscle wastage. Only follow these exercises if your saddle fits correctly. To check whether your saddle is likely to pinch, sit in the saddle and push your fingers right down inside the pommel on either side of your horse's wither. Stand up and move to 3 and 9 o'clock. There should be no hard pressure on your fingers. If there is, postpone this exercise until you can remedy the problem.

Pole position

Making the most of walking a show jumping course can mean the difference between a clear round and frustration. Show jumping trainer Carol Mailer explains how to do it well.

How many times have you come out of the ring having had a fence down or a refusal that spoils an otherwise professional round? Have you ever stopped to wonder whether things could have been different if you had paid more attention to walking the course?

It's impossible to overestimate the importance of walking the course properly. You're the only half of the partnership who gets the chance to preview all the hazards involved, so your horse will be relying on you. There's no dress rehearsal or chance for him to look around. What he sees for the first time is what he will be asked to jump, and you owe it to him to make it as easy as possible to jump a clear round.

Every course builder has his own ways of sorting out the competitors. In novice classes, where the entries are numerous, a well-placed fence going away from the collecting ring will rapidly reduce the number of riders going forwards to the jump-off. Other course builders favour a long run between fences to encourage the rider to be a little too casual and risk having a fence down. Sometimes, a course builder will set a distance that many riders will find difficult to judge, unless they know how to ride a very correct and positive line. In most cases, the riders who go clear will be those who took note of these potential problems before they rode the course.

WALKING THE WALK

When you are invited to walk the course, be smart about it. If you dawdle, you might find you are asked to leave the ring before you've completed the track. Keep your wits about you and limit any conversation to discussing the course you are inspecting.

If your trainer is walking with you, remember that they have much more experience in course walking so listen carefully to every comment they make. If you have nobody to help you, don't be afraid to approach someone more experienced for advice on how to ride a particular fence. Many people will be pleased to help, especially if you ask in a respectful way.

THE FIRST FENCE

A good jump at the first fence will help set the tone for the whole round, so give it plenty of thought.

Most course builders are kind enough to site the first one or two fences heading back towards the collecting ring and exit. This will help to get a slightly reluctant horse or nervous rider over the initial fence. Check the starting gates or beam is positioned so it doesn't cause you to deviate from a straight line as you approach the jump.

Look to see which rein you have to be on as you approach the first jump. If there is a choice, decide which direction you will come from. Plan your approach so that you are absolutely straight, giving your horse every opportunity to see what you want him to jump.

If the arena is large, decide where you will turn to begin your run up. A long, straight approach to the first fence will

Take time to decide how you will approach the first fence

not necessarily give you more time to get it right. In fact, too long an approach will give you more time to get it wrong. Allow yourself at least four or five straight strides to the first obstacle. As you walk through the starting gates, check where fence two is in relation to fence one. If they are in a straight line, then a wise rider will check the distance between the jumps to see if it will suit their horse.

Also bear in mind the type of fence ahead. If the second fence is in a line and is an inviting staircase fence, you can plan to allow the horse to go forward a little more. If there is a stark upright or square parallel coming up, you would be wise to steady a touch and remember to give the horse a little more time to fold his legs out of the way.

GOING THE DISTANCE

Generally, the course builder will use a conventional distance between fences (related distance), particularly in novice classes. Each stride usually measures 12'. You should practise your horse's length of stride at home, so that you're aware of any adjustments you need to make if a related distance doesn't suit him.

If you have done your homework, related distances should be simple for any rider who maintains the correct rhythm and impulsion between the fences. Occasionally the course builder might set an unconventional distance (either deliberately or by mistake). You must be prepared to make an extra adjustment between such fences, if necessary, to give your horse every opportunity to please you.

The big picture

The course plan shown is typical of many novice tracks and incorporates most of the problems you are likely to meet.

However straightforward the course may look, it deserves to be walked exactly on the line you mean to take. If you cut the corners on your own feet, then your horse will probably do the same.

Top tip
■ When calculating a related distance, always allow 6' for the landing and 6' for the take–off. For example, a 24' distance would take one stride and a 60' distance would be four strides

Take care when working out your strides

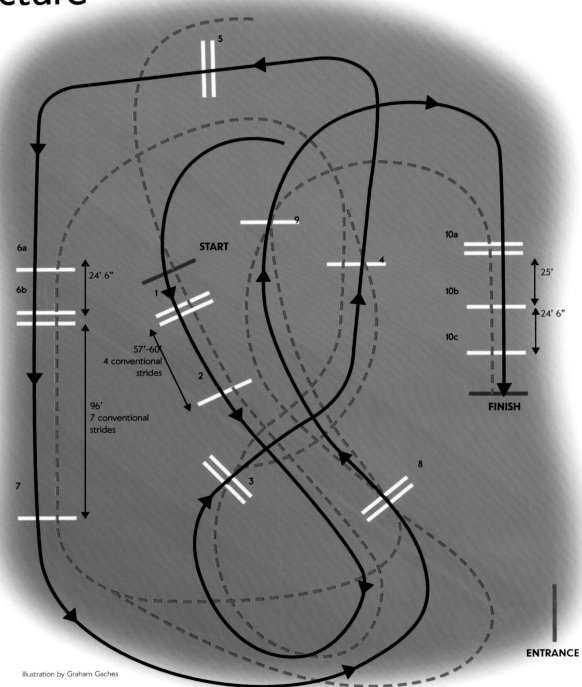

Illustration by Graham Gaches

Here's how to walk this course:

Fence one and two
Decide your approach to fences one and two and sort out the striding between the fences. Walk the track to number three as you mean to ride it. If your horse is a little green or nappy, plan to give him some extra encouragement as you go past the entrance so there is no loss of concentration or reluctance to go forward.

Fence three
Fence three is a parallel, so walk squarely up to it along the route you mean to ride. Recognise how easy it would be to allow your horse to cut the corner and jump slightly off-centre, giving you a poor approach to number four.

Fence four
Fences three and four are not in line and the turn to number four should be walked carefully. If you walk a correct line, the distance should suit your horse. If you curve in or curve out too wide, you might meet number four on a half stride, which will not help. Walk squarely away from number three, then, when you think you need to turn to number four, make it a positive change of direction, remembering to count your paces. This way, when you ride it, you will know how many strides to take before you turn your horse to the jump. If you walk the turn and meet number four on the wrong distance, walk it again until you can decide how many straight strides you need to take and when to turn to get the best line.

Fence five
As you walk, don't be tempted to cut inside number five. Even very experienced riders have been known to miss out a jump, particularly an isolated one at the end of the arena. Sometimes you are concentrating so hard on the next fence which you feel could be more difficult, like the double at number six, that number five can be forgotten. Don't fall into that trap.

Fence six
The course builder has been kind on this course, as the double and treble (fence 10) combinations are both heading back to the friendly end of the arena. You must still walk the line to numbers 6a and 6b exactly as you hope to ride them. If you cut in and approach 6a on the angle as you walk, it will be easy to be a little casual when you ride. Pace the distance between the double accurately. You should know from practice the difference a few inches can make on a one-stride distance, so decide now if you will need to push on or go steady on the non-jumping stride.

Fence seven
Fence six is followed by another related distance, which you need to get clear in your mind. Pace the distance accurately so you know how many strides you want to take. Because it is a longer distance, you have more room for adjustment. The course builder has set the distance to seven conventional strides. You are jumping towards home and your horse might accelerate a bit, so plan what to do.

Number seven is a set of planks, so you need to think about the approach as you walk. There should be no problem with the steering, as it is in a straight line, but your horse might be onward bound and it would be most unwise to be sailing too fast to a set of planks. Remind yourself to settle the horse as soon as you've landed after fence six.

If your horse is stuffy, you can plan to steady and ride a slightly shorter stride and take the planks on eight strides instead of seven.

Here the course builder is using an obvious ploy to cut down on the number of clear rounds. Your horse will be heading back to the collecting ring, and may not be keen on the idea of carrying on past the corner to another fence directly away from his friends. Walk a route that tries to avoid too much confrontation and don't walk too close to the exit. Plan to be positive as you approach the corner and decide exactly where you might need to give an extra little bit of encouragement.

Fence nine
Number eight leads to another dogleg approach across to nine, so remind yourself as you walk that you need to look where you mean to go. Do exactly as you did from three to four. Walk the route and decide how many straight strides to take away from number eight before you turn to square up to number nine.

Fence 10
It would be easy to cut the corner to number 10 and neglect to check your approach. You need to be able to see the combination as your horse will see it. There might be something odd that will distract him and catch you out. If you approach the fence as he will, you will see any pitfalls and be ready for them.

When you pace the distance between the elements, be aware that you will be jumping in over a parallel. If he is prone to putting in a bigger jump over a spread, you need to check how much room there is to the next fence so you can steady him accordingly. In novice classes, the distance should not take you by surprise but sometimes, if the jumps are small, the distance can seem a bit long. This is when you must be sure of the length of your own stride.

The finish line
One last thing – make sure you go through the finish. It would be very easy to duck under the ropes after walking number 10. Big mistake! Although the finish gates are usually in line with the last fence, sometimes, the course builder can set them on an angle. It is not uncommon for a rider to miss going through the finish, purely because they have relaxed too soon and left the horse to take his own line home.

A final glance
Before you leave the ring, have a last look round to remind yourself about how you plan to ride it. Although things can very quickly go wrong once you and the horse are actually jumping, the prior knowledge you have acquired will certainly help you out if the unexpected happens. Just stay cool, let your forward-planning come into play and reap the rewards.

You owe it to your horse to walk the course well

Dressage - you can do it!

If you want to try a dressage test but don't know where to begin - give yourself a head start with a dressage competition workshop and find out what the judge expects.

For many riders, the thought of entering a dressage competition can be terrifying and daunting. It's just you and your horse having to remember and perform complicated movements under the scrutiny of a critical judge. A hack in the countryside sounds much more fun. However, dressage is good for you and your horse. The schooling you need for a basic test will help in all other areas of your riding, including jumping and obedience on the road. And you don't have to be Carl Hester to have a go – any rider and any horse can try a basic dressage test.

New one-day British Dressage Competition Workshops are aimed at encouraging riders to try dressage. The courses will cover everything you need to know from what to wear to what the judge will be looking for. You can take your own horse and there will be the chance to ride a test in front of a judge. By the end of the day, you will have the confidence to get out there, have a go and enjoy yourself!

WHERE TO START

The first level of affiliated dressage tests is called Preliminary. Each test has a number and the lower the number, the easier the test. For example, Preliminary 2 is more straightforward than Preliminary 18. If you are schooling your horse at home in walk, trot, canter and ride basic school movements, such as 20m circles and serpentines, you are doing all that is asked for in a Preliminary test.

At this level the judge is looking for you and your horse to have the basics of training in place, with the emphasis on rhythm, suppleness and contact. You should have a good balanced position, be able to follow your horse's movement, maintain a light elastic contact with your horse's mouth and apply clear aids effectively and without unnecessary movement.

Your horse should have regular, unhurried paces, be obedient to the aids and accept a rein contact without resistance or tension. He should move forward willingly with active hindquarters and remain reasonably straight.

THE PACES

Walk

Walk is a marching pace with a four-time beat. At Prelim level you are required to show two walks:

■ **Medium walk** Your horse should walk calmly with his hind feet overtracking his front. (This is when the imprint of the back foot falls in front of the imprint left by the front foot on the same side). The judge will be looking for a good even, four-time rhythm with both hindlegs taking equal sized steps. You will receive lower marks for changes in rhythm, breaking into trot or if he becomes hollow

■ **Free walk on a long rein** This is usually carried out across a long diagonal. Your horse's steps should increase in length. He should reach forward and down, but remain round as you allow your reins to become longer. Often the walk that you see at the end of the test as the horse leaves the arena is what the judge is looking for

Trot

At this first level of dressage you are required to show working trot and you can sit or rise during the test. In a good working trot the horse is working forwards equally into both reins in an even rhythm. The horse should be pushing himself from his hindquarters with little weight on his shoulders. The judge will be looking for the horse's head to be slightly in front of the vertical. If you draw an imaginary line, which is perpendicular to the ground, down the front of your horse's nose, his head should be slightly in front of this line, but not behind it.

If you carry a whip it is not necessary to keep changing hands each time you change the rein. Decide which hand you are going to use to carry your whip and keep it there. Also, if you decide to rise to the trot, try to ride on the correct diagonal. You won't be penalised for not doing this but you are trying to create a good impression for the judge, not draw attention to your weak areas.

Riding Advice

Canter

At Prelim level you will be asked to show working canter. The judge will be looking for a correct strike-off into canter with a clear, even three-beat rhythm. You need to ensure you remain in canter for the duration of the movement you are asked to perform.

TRANSITIONS

A big part of riding a dressage test is accuracy. You will be asked to carry out transitions to walk, trot and canter at various points around the arena. You should try to achieve these transitions as your knee is level with the required marker. The judge will be looking to see good preparation beforehand. At prelim level the judge is looking to see aids being given correctly and the horse responding accordingly.

MOVEMENTS

The movements you will be asked to do are fairly basic, but it is important you ride them accurately. For example, your circles should not have any straight lines. The judge will be looking to see that your horse stays in a correct rhythm for the pace he is in. You will be marked down for circles that are too big or small. Odd shaped circles will also receive lower marks. Your horse should be bending throughout his body in the direction of the circle, if he has a tendency to look outwards then you will not gain extra marks. Practising correct circles at home will make it much easier when you come to ride them in a test.

Mark out a 20m circle in your schooling area using cones to mark out the four points of the circle. For example, if you are riding a 20m circle right at B, point 1 is at B, point 2 is on the centre line midway between X and A, point 3 is at E and point 4 is midway between X and C (see the diagram right). Ride to each of these four points on a curve. You could also put down a track of sand or shavings marking out the circle.

You may be asked to ride a serpentine from A or C. This consists of half-circles connected by straight lines. In a 20m x 40m arena you will normally be asked to ride a three-loop serpentine (see diagram right). The judge will want to see that your horse remains supple through the changes of bend and maintains his rhythm at all times.

Riding the centre lines

The start and finish of all tests will involve riding up the centre line towards the judge. At the beginning of the test your priority is to be straight. If you are crooked, or wobble about up the centre line, the judge will mark you down. To ride a centre line well, it is essential that your horse is moving forwards from your legs into an even rein contact.

At the end of the test you will ride up the centre line again before halting and saluting. Keep looking ahead, this will also help you stay straight. The transition to halt can be progressive, showing a few steps of walk first. Then halt, but ride forwards to the halt and don't just drift into it.

The salute at the end of the test is done by putting your reins and whip into one hand and dropping the other hand back behind the thigh, then lowering your head in a nod.

Leaving the arena

Each test requires you to leave the arena at A on a long rein. Remember, this is still part of the test. After the halt and salute you should walk towards C and then turn left or right, and make your way diagonally to A. Your horse should walk out calmly, stretching his head and neck downward.

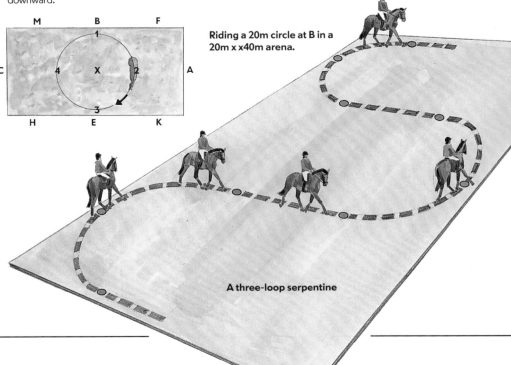

Riding a 20m circle at B in a 20m x x40m arena.

A three-loop serpentine

SCORING

You are awarded marks out of 10 for each set of movements in the test. As you ride the test the judge gives comments which are written on your score sheet. You can collect your score sheet at the end of the competition. These give you good information on where you did well and what areas may need a bit of work in order to get better marks in the future.

The judge awards further marks out of 10 called collective marks. There are four areas: paces (freedom and regularity); impulsion (the desire to move forwards, elasticity of steps and suppleness of the back); submission (acceptance of the aids, confidence, balance, lightness and ease of movements); rider's position and seat: correctness and effect of the aids. Here the judge will award marks for the overall impression of the test in the four areas.

The marks are then added together to give you an overall score which is also converted into a percentage. Ideally you should be aiming to achieve 50% in your tests and improving each time you compete. **Thanks to Knights End Farm, Dan Odell and Dr Amanda Turner's horse, Ofontaine.**

FIND OUT MORE

British Dressage (BD) Competition Workshops will be taking place all over the country and are open to anyone. Each day will cater for a maximum of eight people, divided into two groups of four. If you are unable to get your horse to the venue you can attend dismounted. To find out more, contact British Dressage on 024 7669 8839 or visit www.britishdressage.co.uk

Top tip

You don't need access to an arena, to practise dressage. You can improvise in your paddock at home. Pace out a 20m x 40m rectangular area, placing markers at the relevant points (use the diagram, below left, as a guide and put a cone at each of the letter markers).

To make it easier for you and your horse, mark each corner of the area using pieces of upturned guttering (see pic above).

You've decided to enter your first dressage competition. Follow our 10 steps to make it a success.

We have showed you what you need to practise if you are planning to ride a Preliminary dressage test. Now you've fine-tuned all the movements and you're ready to ride in front of a judge, use our 10–point plan to make your competition day as stress free as possible.

1 ENTERING THE COMPETITION

Once you have a copy of the competition schedule for the show you are planning to enter, read through it carefully. Have a look at the tests to see whether they are suitable for you and your horse's level of training.

If you don't have a copy of the test, send 30p per sheet and an SAE to: British Dressage, NAC, Stoneleigh Park, Kenilworth, Warwickshire CV8 2RJ. Post this in plenty of time and they will send copies of the relevant sheets.

Fill in the entry form clearly, send the right amount of money and return it before the closing date. If you miss the closing date, call the secretary and ask if she will still accept entries. You should be prepared to pay a late entry fee.

2 PHONING FOR TIMES

Each competitor is allocated a time to ride their test. Usually, you have to ring the organiser a few days before the competition who will tell you what time you have been given. Check the schedule for details of when to do this. Under British Dressage rules, if you fail to ring for your times you may be deemed to have withdrawn.

3 LEARNING THE TEST

At Preliminary level a helper (caller) is allowed to read the test to you when you are riding in front of the judge. It is your responsibility to find a caller, not the competition organiser's. Ask a friend if they will call for you. Practise at home so she gets a feel for how fast and how loud to read the test. You should try to learn the test so you are not totally dependent on your caller.

There are lots of ways to learn dressage tests and it's down to you to find the best way for you. You can draw it on paper or walk it on foot in your arena or living room. You can buy wipe–clean boards with blank arenas marked out onto which you can draw your test.

Take a copy of the test to a lesson with your instructor and work on any areas of concern. Also ride through the test a couple of times to check that you can remember it. If your horse anticipates movements after several repetitions, it may be wise just to ride sections of the test and save putting it all together until the big day.

4 WHAT TO WEAR

Wear your competition clothing before the day to make sure it's comfortable and fits properly. Make a list of all the gear you need to take with you.

You are allowed to wear:
- Black or navy jacket or hacking jacket with a stock or shirt and tie
- White, cream or beige jods or breeches
- Gloves must be worn – avoid bright colours which draw attention to your hands
- Long boots (black or brown)
- Jodhpur boots and gaiters
- You must wear a hat whenever mounted
- You can wear spurs and carry a whip

Your horse is allowed to wear:
- A plain leather snaffle bridle with a drop, cavesson or flash noseband
- An English saddle – GP or dressage style
- A plain numnah (avoid bright colours)
- A breastplate but not a martingale
- Boots or bandages when warming up only

Top tip

If your horse gets excited, allow time to ride him twice before your test. Ride or lunge (check with the organiser) for 20 minutes, then put him back in the box before getting him out again to warm-up for the test

5 BE PREPARED

Once you have the time of your test you can start to plan your day. Work back from your test time, adding on your warm-up and preparation time. Allow for tacking up and getting changed etc. Also, give yourself time to find the secretary, the toilets and the warm-up area.

Next, consider the journey. Always allow extra time in case there are any hold-ups en-route. If possible, have a dummy run in your car so you know where you are going. There is nothing worse than arriving late and having to rush. This will put both you and your horse on edge.

Preliminary classes are normally the first of the day, so bear this in mind before you enter if you are planning to travel any distance.

6 THE DAY BEFORE

Pack all your gear, ticking each item off your checklist.

It is not necessary to plait your horse but you are trying to create a good impression, so it is important for both of you to be neat and tidy. If you do plait up it's a good idea to do it the night before. This will save you time in the morning, especially if you have an early start.

7 ON ARRIVAL

When you arrive at the competition go to the secretary and collect your number. Take time to find out where the warm-up area is and whether the competition is running to time. Take a minute to get your bearings and locate the toilets.

8 WARMING UP

This is your time to warm-up your horse ready for your test. It is not the time to start schooling. You are aiming to get his muscles warm and make him as relaxed as possible in his new surroundings.

If possible, start your warm-up by walking round for a few minutes in walk on a long rein. Then, still on a long rein, move forward to rising trot round the edge of the warm-up area. After five to 10 minutes, start to shorten your reins and ride with more of a contact. Introduce lots of transitions to get your horse listening to your aids. Make regular changes of rein and ride serpentines which have frequent changes of bend to help supple your

horse and get him listening and responding to your aids.

About five minutes before you are due to enter the arena, visualise riding your test so the movements are clear in your mind.

9 BEFORE YOU START

The steward will call you when it is your turn and you can ride round the outside of the arena before you enter. Introduce your horse to anything spooky at this point. For example, ride past the judge's car on both reins so he is familiar with it before you start your test.

10 KEEP BREATHING AND SMILE

When the judge signals you to begin, she will sound her car horn or ring a bell. Don't panic. You have 60 seconds to start, don't delay for too long and remember to make a good first impression. Circle near A, make a good turn and ride up the centre line. And smile!

Preparation is the key to a good test

Riding in harmony

Classical and remedial trainer Heather Moffett explains why a good position will enhance your riding enjoyment and relationship with your horse.

A rider with a correct classical position and quiet aids, that are clear to the horse yet not visible to the onlooker, is a joy to watch. Such a rider moves with the horse, not against him and the overall picture is one of harmony, mutual respect and understanding. A good position and clear aids make it easier for your horse to do the things you ask. This leads to fewer misunderstandings and ultimately, a better relationship with your horse, whether you enjoy a quiet hack at the weekends or aspire to top–class competitions.

I feel strongly that riders with poor positions can cause their horses discomfort and this leads to behavioural problems. I am in very much in favour of the equine behaviour features that have appeared in magazines in the last few years. However, I think that if riders improved their riding, and therefore did not hinder their horse's natural movement, many of these behavioural problems would never arise.

Heather Moffett has taught riding for nearly 30 years, lecturing and instructing in the UK and overseas. She is well known for pioneering logical, simple methods of riding and training. Her own classical training has been with Desi Lorent and Dr Margaret Cox.
For details of seminars and workshops with Heather, visit www.enlightenedequitation.com

THE CLASSICAL SEAT

Riders regularly ask me why it is so important to spend time developing their seat. It's a common misconception that this is simply not necessary for riders who just hack out or aren't interested in dressage. The primary purpose of a classical seat, is to allow the horse to function unhindered underneath the rider. In my opinion, this should be the aim of everyone who sits on a horse.

The classical seat developed because the old masters found that it was the only position in which they could easily influence the horse, and it also permitted the use of subtle, discreet aids.

Classical riders have a longer leg position, a tall upright torso and the desire to sit as still and quietly as possible. I think it's interesting that we can also see this position in the horse-men of the Iberian peninsula and Western riders. The Australian stock saddle actually encourages a good classical position. These riders all spend long hours in the saddle and need to have a position that is less tiring for both horse and rider, while allowing the greatest control with the least effort.

When hunting became popular in this country, riders soon found that the classical position was impractical across country and began to develop a position which became known as the hunting or chair seat.

It wasn't until the last century that thinking began to alter and, with the emergence of dressage as a sport in the UK, riders began to adopt the more upright line of balance. Unfortunately, many saddlers have not realised this fact and are still making saddles that put riders in the hunting seat (pic below left). I think this is the reason that so many riders struggle to maintain their alignment.

In general, most instructors will teach that the ear/shoulder/hip/heel line is the position of balance, and that is what we should all be aiming for. This is often explained by saying that if the horse and saddle were whisked away, you would land in a standing position with the knees slightly bent. If you tip forward you would land on your nose, and if you leaned back you would land on your rear end.

Many GP saddles encourage the chair or hunting seat

The correct ear/shoulder/hip/ankle alignment

THE EQUISIMULATOR

I am lucky in that for the last few years I have had the use of a wonderful machine, the Equisimulator, developed for me by a friend and student, Jon Heyes. This machine replicates the movement of the horse, allowing me to teach riders to sit correctly and to show them, hands on, the exact movements required to sit as one with the horse.

Students can feel the difference between correct and incorrect rider balance

This machine also allows me to graphically demonstrate to students what the horse actually feels. By placing the hand (knuckles uppermost) under the cantle region of the saddle they are left in no doubt as to why the horse functions better with a rider who sits in balance with the movement. When I am riding the machine in the typical chair seat, the hand is well and truly squashed. When I am riding the machine in good balance, the student will hardly feel my weight in the saddle.

If I interact with the Equisimulator in an incorrect way, it demonstrates very powerfully the opposition to its movement. If it does this to a machine, what must it do to a living creature? The machine corrects itself again immediately the rider absorbs the movement in sync.

PUT YOURSELF IN YOUR HORSE'S PLACE

You don't need the Equisimulator to get an idea of what your horse might feel when you ride him. Enlist the help of a friend and try this experiment with a saddle horse and a saddle. Place your hand under the cantle region and get the friend to sit in the correct ear/shoulder/hip/heel line position. Now ask her to collapse her waist and round her back. Note the difference in the pressure you feel on your hand. Then get the friend to lean back and notice the difference in pressure.

There are reflex points under the cantle region which cause the horse's back to dip when pressure is applied. Is it any wonder that it is difficult to get a horse to lift and round, if the rider is sitting in a way which is depressing his back and making him dip, rather than raise it?

SOFTLY, SOFTLY

Quiet discreet aids are just as important when it comes to achieving a harmonious relationship with your horse. When you see the elegance and beauty of the Spanish Riding School, do you notice the riders? I doubt it, because they appear to be doing nothing. We're all too busy looking in awe at the breathtakingly agile and well-schooled horses. When you see a fine show jumper, such as the Whitakers, or my own favourite now retired John Ledingham of Ireland,

making the Hickstead Derby look like a clear round course, it is no different. The horse is balanced between hand and leg and the aids are so refined that it is almost impossible to see them.

You do not see these riders banging away with their heels and legs or yanking the horse in the mouth. Yet you can see this at every show you visit. Far too many riders think force is necessary to control a horse and regularly use it in the belief that it is part of his training.

Good riding principles apply to all disciplines. John Whitaker is a fine example

No worries!

How to improve your riding by using your mind

'Think about what **you've achieved** with your horse, rather than focusing on what you've got left **to learn**.'

Imagine you're out on a hack with a friend. It's a beautiful day. The birds are singing, the sun is warm on your back, a gentle breeze is blowing. You're enjoying spending quality time with your horse.

Riding along, you find yourself peering down a steep drop. For no particular reason you're drawn to it and a scene starts to build in your head. You're picturing what would happen if your horse suddenly slipped. The image of you both landing in a crumpled heap at the bottom of the slope is sharp in your mind.

WHAT IF...

Our vivid imaginations remind us of the situations that scare us. What ifs enter our minds every day. These are the thoughts that can hold us back and spoil our fun. They creep into our heads without us even realising it.

Worrying makes us feel anxious and ultimately makes us miserable. And whether we're worrying about a real problem, or something that our minds have invented, the effect is the same.

However, we have the power to decide whether to fill our heads with positive or negative thoughts. This may seem obvious – but it takes a conscious effort to catch yourself thinking bad things and quickly replace them with something good.

BE HAPPY

We all want to ride the best that we can. Being aware of our weak points helps us to sort them out. But the danger of concentrating on problems is that you can sometimes talk yourself into seeing them as bigger than they really are.

When you're trying to work on something that you struggle with, it's important to remain positive. For example, if you're finding canter transitions difficult, don't convince yourself that you can't do them. Talk to your instructor, look at the problem logically and work out what's going wrong. There are plenty of other people who can ride good transitions, so you can too.

Riders at every level beat themselves up about the way they ride. When things aren't going as well as you'd like, try to remember to look on the bright side. Think about what you have achieved with your horse, rather than only focusing on what you've got left to learn. Struggling with your riding can be very frustrating, but cast your mind back and you will see how much you've improved without even noticing. You'll feel better about yourself, and it will show in your riding.

MIND OVER MATTER

If you're worried about doing something, whether it's a competition or successfully going out on a hack, picturing yourself doing it well can really help. Practise in your mind when there's nothing to distract you, a good time is when you're falling asleep. Ride through your dressage test or cross-country course in your head. Ride every step, but only think about it going well. It's important you don't allow any negative thoughts to creep in.

When you're on your horse, learn to recognise what happens when you're getting yourself worked up. If you find yourself feeling flustered take a deep breath. Don't panic!

'When you beat your fears, worries and anxieties, you'll find they are replaced with satisfaction'

It can often help you to ride more positively if you imagine you're riding like someone you look up to. If you admire the way a top dressage rider sits so perfectly, or how a great event rider, even someone you know, has such determination going into a fence, try to picture yourself in their place.

MANAGING YOUR FEARS

One of the best ways you can become a more positive and confident rider is to pretend that's what you are. So when you start to feel worried, blank it out and tell yourself you're not scared. This doesn't mean you should be reckless, but by pretending you're confident you will become confident and you will start to enjoy yourself more. If you allow yourself to be afraid or indecisive, your horse will sense it and believe there is truly something to worry about.

As you learn that bad things aren't going to happen your confidence grows until you find that you don't have to pretend any more.

Don't worry

Allowing your mind to conjure up all the bad things that can happen subconsciously chips away at your confidence. This has a negative effect on your riding. For example, you're worried about cantering because you think you'll lose control. Your horse feels that you're nervous. You start to grip and he gets tense. This just makes you more worried, which makes him more worried, and so it goes on.

When you catch yourself focusing on negative thoughts – whether it's falling off, or stopping at a jump – try to teach yourself not to do it. By thinking about the worst case scenario you're just terrifying yourself with possibilities.

Speaking at the 2002 Equine Event, top international show jumper Andy Austin emphasised the importance of positive thinking. "The only thing that will stop you getting over a fence is your mind," he said. "If you think you'll have problems, you will."

Even when you are feeling scared it helps if you can tell yourself to push away the negative thoughts and think of something good. If you can practise doing this, you'll come back from your rides feeling a lot happier. Being positive gives you a greater sense of achievement and allows your confidence to grow. Look at beating your fears as a way to improve your riding.

'It can often help you to ride more positively if you imagine you're riding like someone you look up to'

THE FEEL GOOD FACTOR

When you beat your fears, worries and anxieties, you'll find they are replaced with satisfaction. Every small achievement can leave you feeling proud of yourself and your horse.

Try to think about the things that are scaring you and holding you back as a rider. What would you really like to be able to do? If you're worried about jumping, why not face your fears and learn to do some small fences? Don't feel pressured to overstretch yourself to start with, there's no need. Everyone has to start somewhere and it doesn't matter if you only jump the tiniest fence. And remember there's no reason why your horse would suddenly decide to throw himself over the edge of that steep bank.

Pippa Funnell

It's hard to believe that even the most successful riders can struggle with confidence. Sports psychology helped top British event rider and double European gold medal-winner Pippa Funnell to get over her negative thoughts.

"I had a few bad years when I started to lose confidence and lacked self-belief. At competitions I was relaxed about the dressage, but when it came to cross-country I got nervous. The more I walked the course, the more I imagined the jumps getting bigger, wider and harder.

Getting involved in sports psychology really helped me to think positively. It allowed me to to channel my thoughts positively.

When you're preparing for a big competition you can't afford to leave a stone unturned. You have to think positively. Now I've learnt to be completely focused.

When I'm preparing to go cross-country I give myself 20 minutes on the day when I ride through the course in my head. Now I've got a system, I can think logically, where in the past my nerves tended to take over."

Anky van Grunsven

All top riders have their own ways of coping with nerves and, although she has ridden at hundreds of competitions, Olympic dressage gold medallist Anky van Grunsven says she still gets a little tense before a test or a demonstration.

"At a competition I never try to do something that I can't do at home because it's always going to be more difficult at a competition. Your level at home should always be more than your level at the competition."

Anky describes herself as an optimist and thinks her outlook on life helps. "If you want to compete I think you have to be an optimistic person. Some people see a glass that's half-empty, mine is always half-full. I do have my downs but I don't stay there. When I heard that one of my best horses, Joker, was injured it was a bad time, but when things like that happen you have to find something positive."

Anky's tip

■ Anky's friend Peter Murphy, a former national volleyball coach for The Netherlands, helps her with sports psychology. One of his tips is to avoid setting goals that are targeted on results. He believes that performance goals are better, eg to aim to ride as well as possible and enjoy it, rather than riding to win.

Secrets of dressage success

There's more to dressage than simply learning a series of movements. Nikki Routledge finds out what qualities the judge is looking for, and reveals the five most common faults to affect your score and how to avoid them.

Dressage is a French word that many of us use every day, but the full meaning of it is often overlooked. It is a word usually associated with a horse's training but it can also be used to describe the total improvement of the horse.

Dressage judge and trainer Julie Box believes that this total improvement comes through the daily use of gymnastic exercises to improve your horse's physical strength and develop greater impulsion. Mentally, your horse should become obedient to you, based on a relationship of co-operation and consistent communication. In her teaching, Julie cites French classical rider Captain Beudant, who said, "Ask for much, be content with little and reward often."

Many people think of dressage as

teaching your horse to perform specific movements, but it is as much about developing his physical strength, balance and stamina. In human terms, it is similar to swimmers who use weight-lifting exercises as well as swimming to improve their body fitness and stamina and this, in turn, improves their swimming style.

You should include transitions, school movements and lateral exercises in your dressage programme, so your horse gains the physical strength and ability to work with balance, suppleness and in self-carriage.

Each movement in a dressage test is reflective of a training idea, which is evaluated by the judge watching you. Rather than viewing the competition as an end in itself, you should look at it as a way of assessing you and your horse's progress in your dressage at home.

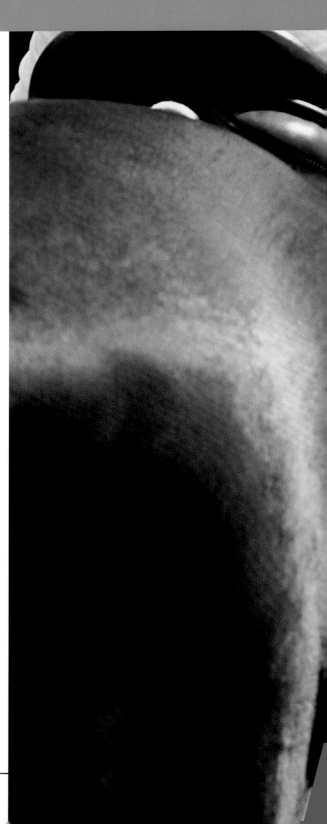

Nikki Routledge PGD, BSc (Hons), BHSAI, EBW is a McTimoney animal therapist and equinology body worker. She treats horses and dogs with movement and/or performance problems and gives advice on correct exercise programmes. She also teaches animal massage and competes in endurance on her horse. For more information, visit Nikki's website: www.horsesanddogs.co.uk

What the judge will look for?

Whether you're working your horse at home or at a competition, there are a number of qualities you should aim to achieve. These include relaxation, balance, rhythm, tempo, impulsion, suppleness and engagement. Here, Julie explains what each of these mean:

RELAXATION

"When a horse is relaxed and engaged he will produce longitudinal flexion, which is often called being on the bit. This means he is rounding his back, lifting his hindlegs under his body and working through to the bridle. He is submissive to the forward–driving aids given by the rider."

BALANCE

"In competition, the judge will be looking to see if the last step of a gait (canter, for example) is as clear and balanced as the first step of the new gait (trot, for example). If the steps of the gait deteriorate before the horse falls into the new one, then balance is missing."

RHYTHM AND TEMPO

"The rhythm and tempo should be consistent throughout. Any change of rhythm is an evasion by your horse. By increasing or decreasing the tempo, your horse is avoiding engagement of his hindquarters as well as lateral flexion, as he needs that lateral flexion to engage."

IMPULSION

"This is achieved by gradually encouraging increased flexion and movement in the joints of the haunches. This way, you can teach your horse to move with greater animation, yet with decreased speed. Speed is the enemy of impulsion."

SUPPLENESS

"Suppleness is the effect of your horse moving fluently, with a round back and flexed joints."

ENGAGEMENT

"This occurs when the haunches accept the majority of the weight, with a lifting of the forehand. Daily exercises to increase engagement will ultimately produce collection and extension of your horse's natural paces."

Five common faults

In Preliminary and Novice tests, the judge will be evaluating your horse's straightness, suppleness and ability to go forward from the aids. He should clearly demonstrate relaxation, rhythm and obedience in your test. Julie reveals the five common faults seen in tests at this level and how you can avoid them:

Most horses find bending one way easier than the other

To correct crookedness, aim to move the shoulders in line with the quarters

1 CROOKED OR NOT STRAIGHT

"Most horses are naturally 'banana shaped' and will find bending one way easier than the other," says Julie. "Your horse needs to be straight in order for you to develop suppleness (and vice versa), so that the weight can be carried evenly over his limbs.

"To correct any crookedness, you need to bring the shoulder in, place the inside foreleg in front of the inside hindleg and maintain this position using your outside rein. You can do this by using the aids for shoulder-in: if you are on a circle, keep a contact with your outside rein, soften with the inside rein, keep the outside leg back and use your inside leg on the girth. The aim is to move the shoulders over in line with the quarters, rather than vice versa. Riding shoulder-in on the long side of the school will correct your horse if his quarters swing out, and will also improve his strength. Your halts will get better and your horse will step underneath his body more evenly.

"A crooked horse can't straighten all at once – it will take time and repetition. Crookedness can be a manifestation of uneven development of the muscles and, if not corrected, later, the joints."

2 ABOVE THE BIT OR NOT ON THE BIT

"'On the bit' is a potentially misleading term. Only a horse who accepts the contact and moves forwards to it is athletically correct," explains Julie. "Stretching over the back rounds the top line and enables your horse to move in his entirety, rather than just moving his legs. If the rider holds the horse in a fixed position with her hands, the horse will respond by stiffening the muscles and then the joints, which will ultimately result in deterioration of the paces and choppy, shuffling strides.

"To remedy this, try to work your horse as a supple connection from the hindlegs, over the back and into a secure contact, not just as a shape."

Holding the horse in a fixed shape will result in a shuffling stride

He must accept the contact and move forward

3 RUNNING OR HURRYING

"If you get this comment on your sheet, you need to slow down your horse using repeated half-halts in order to achieve a submissive contact. To ride a good half-halt in trot, indicate the desire to walk and, just before your horse walks, yield with your reins without losing the contact so he is allowed to trot on slowly. Eventually your horse will relax, find his balance and gently accept the contact on the bit."

4 BEHIND THE BIT

"Lazy, weak or young horses will often go behind the bit, rejecting the contact by over-flexing the neck," says Julie (see left). "While he may appear relaxed, your horse will continue to push forward from the hindlegs rather than lifting his weight, and this will prevent the hindlegs coming through properly, causing him to flatten and remain on the forehand.

"To correct this, drive your horse forward to encourage him to take a contact. Entice him to seek the contact by stretching his neck and, as soon as he does so, lighten your hand to make the contact more pleasurable. At the same time, use your leg aids to activate his hindleg and encourage him to take the rein forward."

If your horse is behind the bit, encourage him forward to seek the rein contact

5 NEEDS MORE LATERAL SUPPLENESS

"I use exercises such as shoulder-in and leg-yield every day to improve my own horses. Without lateral suppleness, faults will soon become apparent and, as you progress through the various levels, lateral suppleness becomes more and more important. Typical faults caused by lack of lateral suppleness include interrupted rhythm and your horse stepping through unevenly or stepping out to avoid the bend on turns and circles," explains Julie.

SEVEN STEPS TO IMPROVING YOUR DRESSAGE

1 Think of your horse as an athlete. He should be fit, supple and physically capable of doing what you want. You can achieve this through daily progressive training, but these qualities cannot be forced as and when you need them.

2 Always think from your horse's quarters. Riders often focus on the front end alone, and think of being 'on the bit' as a fixed position. However, being truly on the bit involves a supple connection from the hindleg, over the back and into a secure contact. It is not just a shape.

3 Work with your horse as a partner and friend. If there is a problem in your training and competition performance, it is probably being caused by a communication difficulty rather than your horse trying to be awkward. Aim to solve your problems in a harmonious way.

4 If you are secure in the knowledge that this quality has been correctly developed, it will always shine through.

5 Take time to study the classical riders and aim to develop a greater understanding of your horse and his training needs. Remember that all of us are continuing to learn new things throughout our lives.

6 Never think of a dressage test as an end result, or learn movements simply because you are riding them in a test next week. The movements are in the test for a reason, which is to demonstrate a specific level of training.

7 Be happy with your performance. If you feel your horse has performed well, be satisfied. Winning or being placed is just the icing on the cake.

Lightening the load

Using your body effectively will give your horse the freedom to perform better – and it may even save him from discomfort and injury. Johanna Sharples explains how it's done.

Learning to ride well is a lifelong obsession for many of us, and the quest for improvement can sometimes be a frustrating one. It's all too easy to get bogged down in technicalities, and convince yourself that if only you had an indoor school... a new saddle... lessons with that instructor, everything would fall into place.

The answer is often much more simple, however, and it doesn't always require extra facilities or even a horse! Riders come in all shapes and sizes, and the physically disabled can and do achieve absolute harmony with their horses right up to grand prix level. It's just a question of learning to use your body – or, in some cases, learning not to use it!

"Riding in **harmony** is about learning to **get out** of your horse's way"

LET IT BE

"Riding in harmony is about learning to get out of your horse's way," says classical dressage trainer Marjorie Armstrong. "Learn to be a human being rather than a human doing.

"One of my students only has one arm and she didn't have any trouble riding movements like a soft, flowing half-pass with correct bend, or teaching her horse piaffe in-hand. In the absence of a second arm, she learned to find other solutions and use her body and weight better instead. Her horse was so light and soft in his jaw, too – because she couldn't grab, neither did he.

"Some years ago, I had another student who was totally paralysed down the left side, and could successfully ride shoulder-in in walk and trot on a trained horse."

It's a simple equation: if you can learn to use your body correctly, your horse will be able to use his. It's all about striking a balance – literally.

A disabled rider who may be unable to grip is a good example of someone who has found a way of staying on board which doesn't rely on strength or tension – yes, balance again! The good news is that it's mostly a matter of technique rather than talent, and as such can be learned by all of us.

THE POWER OF POSTURE

When you stand and move around in your daily life, you're not conscious of carrying your own bodyweight. Provided you have good posture, the design of your body allows it to happen without too much effort, otherwise we'd all spend our lives feeling exhausted.

It's the same for your horse. We school horses into maintaining a particular outline because a good outline is a sign of good posture, and it's the healthiest way for him to use his body and cope with carrying your weight.

This only works if the load applied is in good alignment and well balanced, however. If not, the horse's development will reflect the faulty alignment of his load, ie you! Bone, muscle and ligaments will change in a way which leads to the horse misusing his body, causing at best loss of performance and, at worst, serious discomfort and injury. Therefore, the primary focus of your schooling should not necessarily be to get the horse in an outline but to get yourself in a good outline!

ALIGN THAT SPINE

"There are many ways of 'stacking up' your body parts over the foundation of your pelvis, but the only way to do it with true balance is to keep the spine perfectly aligned," says American trainer and physical therapist Anne Howard.

"Correct spinal curves allow you to maintain a good position with minimal tension. They also help the spine to withstand the compressive forces of riding, thus minimising the chance of injury and stress by distributing the forces of gravity evenly through the entire body. It's important to realise that this posture is a dynamic, springy one, not a rigid pose."

It's not easy to change the habits of a lifetime but it is possible if you work on it. The first step is to recognise what you are doing in order to correct it, and become aware of how it is influencing your horse.

As you move around you are not conscious of carrying your bodyweight

QUESTIONS TO ASK YOURSELF

Q Are you tense?

The effect of tension anywhere in a rider's body is quite remarkable. For the horse, it's a bit like trying to drive with the handbrake on. Tension puts a block on the natural shock-absorbing properties of your joints, making it almost impossible to sit softly.

When you jump from a fence to the ground, how do you absorb the shock? By flexing your ankles, knees and hips as you land, because jumping from a height to the ground with straight legs would almost certainly cause pain and injury.

If you have access to a mini trampoline, try the following exercise. Stand with feet hip-width apart, relax your shoulders and, with slight flexions of your knees, start to bounce gently. It takes hardly any effort to get the momentum going, but you need to be relaxed and almost floppy through your body to allow the movement to happen. Tense your leg muscles and see how this puts an immediate brake on the soft bouncing; the same will happen if you tense your shoulders. In fact, the application of tension can be even more subtle; simply close your fists hard or grit your teeth and see the effect it has on the rest of your body.

Q Are you stable?

When it comes to maintaining good posture and balance on or off a horse, core stability is where it's at. If you aren't strong and stable in the core of your being (abdominals, pelvic area and lower back), you'll be activating other muscles to pull you back into balance all the time, and this is the route to tension and imbalance.

Think about how you would hold your trunk if you invited someone to poke your stomach. That's the kind of firmness we're aiming for. Sucking in the tummy and lifting the chest, which is what many of us do when we think about posture, has a completely different feel and actually weakens you at your core.

Q Are you even?

"We all talk of having sensitive hands and using them equally, but having a sensitive seat with your weight evenly distributed across both seatbones and into both thighs is arguably even more important from the horse's point of view," says Anne. She suggests the following exercises to gain seatbone awareness:
■ Sitting on a hard chair, check to see if you can feel each seatbone clearly by sitting on your hands, palms down (pic 1). Is your weight distributed 50% on each seatbone? Do they feel even under you or is the placement on a diagonal line? Does the shape and feel of them seem the same, or does one feel pointier and one feel rounder? What do you need to shift to get them as close to 50:50 as possible? Don't just focus on wiggling your seat to equalise them; try tipping your head or moving your ribs and shoulders as you explore the possibilities
■ Learning to gain control of your own lateral bend is a useful tool when riding. Sit to the side of the chair so that only one seatbone is supported. First, let the non-supported seatbone drop down so that the trunk elongates on that side (pic 2). Your upper body will need to curve over the supported side to stay in balance.

Then lift up the unsupported seatbone, higher than the level of the chair, shortening that side so the curve of the body is to the unsupported side (pic 3). Do this slowly, repeating a few times on one side before trying the same exercise with the other seatbone supported. If you have a helper, ask them to watch your back to see if you get the same number of 'trunk wrinkles' and quality of curve on each side. You might notice that you find it much easier to achieve a curve one way than the other

Q Are you aligned?

"For each person's neutral spine there should be a slight forward curve to the lower back, a slight backward curve through the ribcage, and a very slight forward curve to the neck. A plumb line should drop from the ear, through the shoulder, to the hip," says Anne. To check this, sit on the edge of a hard chair with your feet flat on the floor.

Get a friend to examine your posture from the side and ask the following questions:
1 Do I see three curves to this person's spine – in at the bottom, out over the shoulders and in at the neck? (pic above)
2 Is one curve much larger or dominant?
3 Does the ear-shoulder-hip line fall vertically or does it zig-zag?
4 When I compress the spine, does one of the curves bulge or collapse? Does it feel like a solid structure or a soggy one? Do I sense a lot of muscular guarding in order to hold the position?

1

2

3

COMPRESSION TEST

Get your friend to place her hands on your shoulders, as close as is comfortable to the neck. Her shoulders must be directly over her hands so she can press straight down, without angling forwards or backwards. Ask her to gently press down in a series of three slow down-up-release movements (make sure there is no pain) and ask if she can see a change in the bird's-eye view she has of your trunk. Often, a crease in the belly will become more pronounced (trunk sagging backwards) or the shoulders will move backwards (trunk arching forward). The feel should be very stable, with very little compression and no creases or giving way.

■ Do not compress the head onto the neck

CORRECTING WEAK LINKS

"Few riders have uninjured bodies," says Anne. "Who among us hasn't had at least one good fall? These curves are the ideal, but if you cannot achieve them without discomfort or extreme stress, you might like to think about consulting a good physiotherapist or other body worker."

Play with how much bottom curve you have first, then experiment with the middle backward curve.

■ See if you can sense the difference between saggy and solid. If the lower curve is too flat (not 'swaybacked' enough), the sagging will be a backwards movement in the lower back which may hurt a little. If the bottom curve is too pronounced, the tummy will protrude forward with each compression, the arch will become more pronounced and it may hurt

■ If the middle curve is too flat (one of the most common deviations), you are probably stretching the chest up excessively. In horse terms, this would be hollow-backed and on the forehand!

■ If the middle curve is too rounded try to move so your breastbone is vertical and a bar placed along it would fall vertically to the pubic bone. Ask your friend to give you feedback, as you may not be able to tell by yourself. A mirror would also be useful for this exercise

'The feel you are aiming for is **muscle tone**, not muscle tension. Think **firm** but not stiff, **soft** but not spongy.'

New beginnings

By becoming aware of your asymmetries and correcting them on a daily basis, you'll gradually retrain your muscle memory to stay in a different groove. There are also a number of classes which will help you develop body awareness and better alignment without a horse, such as Feldenkrais method, Alexander Technique, Pilates, T'ai Chi or martial arts-based classes, dance or yoga. Check your local phone book or health club to find out what's available in your area.

Putting yourself right momentarily with the help of a friend is one thing, but staying there is another, and you will need to stabilise your correct foundation with muscle.

Avoid keeping your muscles permanently contracted as all this will do is create tension and make life uncomfortable for yourself and your horse. The feel you are aiming for is muscle tone, not muscle tension. Think firm but not stiff, soft but not spongy.

"Good riders use a high degree of dynamic muscle tone to achieve the quiet, still, relaxed look that we term correct," says Anne. "Compare their look (pic right) to the two postures we often see in beginner riders; either extremely floppy or desperately rigid (pic left) but, in both cases, being moved around by the horse.

"Part of this body style is how good riders produce horses with similar outlines, and how other riders seem to have the same problems on every horse they ride. Recognising and correcting these flaws in position will give you more control over your body and your physical dialogue with the horse."

Compare the quiet, relaxed posture to the extremely rigid one and note the effect it has on the horse

An informed choice

Choosing the right instructor can mean the difference between tears of frustration and tears of joy, so make sure you do your homework, says Tina Sederholm.

Tina Sederholm has taught pupils from novice to international standard for more than 15 years and has competed at international level in horse trials. She is now involved with Coaching the Coaches, a series of lectures in which she blends her equestrian knowledge with her professional presentation techniques in order to show instructors how to teach in a clear, enthusiastic and effective way.

Are you one of the many riders in Britain who only go to an instructor when you have a problem? Or are you one of the few who has an on-going commitment to improve your own riding and your horse's education?

Horses are expensive creatures and sometimes lessons get a rather low priority in the budget. However, most disappointments and frustrations associated with horses come from a lack of understanding, so it makes sense to develop your knowledge in order for you to get the maximum enjoyment from your horse.

Whether you want to feel comfortable hacking or aspire to scale the heights to top–class competition, your riding lessons will provide the backbone of your knowledge. So it is worth taking some time to find the right instructor for you.

GET THE BASICS RIGHT

My belief is that your first priority as a rider is to get a sound basic education. In the past this often happened naturally as people served an apprenticeship as a working pupil with an experienced rider or grew up in a horsey environment. This provided them with an inherent knowledge and feel.

Don't worry if you don't come from a horsey background or didn't ride as a child, it doesn't mean you can't go on to do great things. It may be helpful to stick with one instructor for a while so that you get a consistent philosophy. When you have that in place, you can venture further afield because you have a standard to measure new information against.

Whether you are a beginner or an experienced rider looking for some new challenges, it is worth asking yourself a few questions before you look for an instructor. Try to establish your goals and decide what you want from your lessons. These can be specific, such as wanting to show jump, or more general, such as improving technique or expanding your understanding of horses.

WATCH A LESSON

One of the best ways to find an instructor is to get a personal recommendation from a friend. If possible, go and watch your potential trainer give a lesson. Assess the difference in the horse and rider from the beginning to the end of the lesson. If the instructor is faced with a difficult situation, watch how she deals with it.

Ask yourself: Does this person sound enthusiastic and do I think she will be interested in getting the best from me and my horse? If you have positive answers to these questions, have a trial lesson yourself. If you come away from the lesson feeling you have learned something new, and with increased confidence, the chances are you have found the right person.

TIME FOR A CHANGE?

Sometimes, even when you have been making good progress, learning can become stagnant. At this point, I think it's a good idea to have a lesson with someone else. Fresh ideas can re-ignite your enthusiasm and hearing an idea expressed in a new way can bring clarity where there was confusion.

If you find yourself coming out of your lessons disappointed, it is definitely time to review the situation. You may need a new instructor, but it is also worth asking yourself if you are expecting too much. Many people come with high ambitions, which is fine, but they forget there may be many intermediate steps to achieving that goal. Your instructor is not there to do it for you. It's down to you to put time, effort and, most of all, practice into achieving the goal you have set yourself.

LEARNING IS FUN

Most importantly, pick an instructor who looks upon learning as fun. After all, we got involved with horses in the first place because we like them and they add a special dimension to our lives. The best way to nurture this is to maintain a light-hearted and enthusiastic attitude, and that applies to the pupil, the teacher and the horse.

Plan of action

We school horses because we want to have better communication with them, and have them respond to our requests readily. For me, the well-schooled horse has three basic qualities: He responds willingly to both the forward and controlling aids; he bends and turns softly to the left and right; and he goes on a straight line. The horse is able to fulfil these most successfully if he is well balanced and has a consistent rhythm to his paces. From this foundation, you can teach a horse to do just about anything.

GETTING STARTED

In order to decide what to work on in any given session, it is worth spending the first few minutes assessing what frame of mind you and the horse are in today, and how you both feel physically. Spend four or five minutes riding in walk, trot and canter, while you ask yourself these questions: Is he perky or sluggish? Is he carrying himself well? You also want to check up on your riding. Ask yourself: Do I feel balanced, and am I sitting in the centre of the horse? Am I giving him clear directions? There is little point working on the horse if you are all over the place mentally or physically, so time spent checking your seat and calming your mind will increase the probability of a successful schooling session.

Once you have decided what you want to work on, and how you are going to do it, start the exercise in its simplest form. I start many exercises in walk. Once the horse is responding well to my requests in this pace, I do the exercise in trot, or add another element to make it more of a challenge.

Reward your horse when he does something well. Give him a pat and let him walk on a long rein for a few minutes. This will allow him to recover physically and rest mentally. It also gives you time to think what to do next.

If you are not making headway, it is a good idea to walk on a long rein for a few minutes. This lets your, and the horse's, adrenaline drop, after which you can think calmly about how you could alter your approach. Ask yourself whether you're giving the horse a clear message and whether he's physically able to respond. When you get the solution, you can pick up the reins and start again.

The following exercises are based on being in a 40 x 20m arena, or similar. If your arena is a markedly different size, you will need to make the appropriate adjustments to the places where I have specified certain measurements.

Warm up tips

1 Warming up means getting the horse's muscles up to an optimum working temperature. Therefore when it is cold, you will need slightly more vigorous work, than when the weather is warm.

2 The first couple of minutes can be spent in walk and trot on a long rein. You can then pick up the reins and have the horse in a long frame – with his nose just in front of the vertical, using the whole of the school and making large circles and soft changes of rein in walk, trot and canter.

3 Riders often need more warming up than horses. Scan your body for any stiffness and loosen up that part accordingly. You can even do some stretching exercises before you get on.

4 Use the warm up period to assess yourself and the horse. Is he bright or lazy and is he moving freely?

Riding Advice

EXERCISES FOR ALL HORSES AND RIDERS

The first requirement of any horse is that he goes forward willingly. If he doesn't, you can do very little effective work with him, so a good way to start a schooling session is to test your horse's reaction to your forward aids.

After your initial warm up, bring the horse back to walk. On a long rein, walk around the school and at A, B, C and E ask the horse to lengthen his stride for four or five steps, and then slow him down again. Note the quality of his reactions. Is he willing, or did he put his ears back? Horses get confused when riders push and have tension in their hands at the same time, so testing the horse's reaction to the leg with no contact clarifies that you want him to go forward.

If the horse responds well to this, you can repeat the movement while riding the horse in to a contact. When you push forward, remember to soften the hand a little so the horse knows the door is still open. If the horse is grudging in his reaction, use your voice or give him a

friendly kick when you get to the next marker. Expect him to jump forward. Make sure you give him complete freedom for a few strides so that he knows he is allowed to react positively. Then take him back and give him a pat and, once he has settled, test your lengthening again.

After getting a satisfactory result in walk, change the rein and try the same exercise in trot – lengthen the stride for four or five steps and then collect. You can alter this exercise by forgetting about the lengthening at A and C, and riding the horse 3m inside the track on the long sides. This way, you can test that, when you lengthen at E and B, the horse stays straight.

Each time you get a couple of good reactions, give the horse a change by making some circles of varying sizes. If the horse has been falling out through the left shoulder when you have been doing your lengthening inside the track, work on a left circle so that you make him receptive to your left leg. Then, when you work on straight lines, he will be familiar with responding to your leg when you ask him to stay straight.

If you are getting good forward and

back responses in the trot, try the exercise in canter. Now you can ask the horse to lengthen his canter as soon as you come out of the corner on to the long side. Try this both on and inside the track.

These simple changes of pace introduce a concertina-like feel to the horse and are the basis for larger scale collection and extension. You will also find that the horse is more receptive in transitions.

Although the focus of this session is primarily changes of pace and straightness, intersperse it with some circles and figures of eight so that you give the horse a mental and physical change.

Try lengthening (pic a) and shortening (pic b) the canter stride

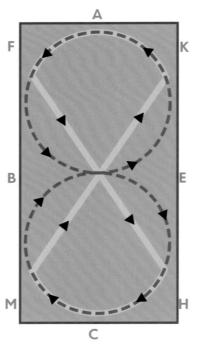

When your horse is responding well to being ridden on a long rein, repeat the exercise, this time riding in to a contact

Make sure you set up the horse for each turn or circle

EXERCISES FOR FRESH OR LAZY HORSES

This is an excellent all-round exercise for training turns and straight lines and making a clear difference between the two. It is called the castle exercise because of its shape – a rectangle with four circles (or turrets), one at each corner (see diagrams, right).

Start as if you were on the left rein, on a line 9m in from the outside track. (This is just a reference point for starting – from now on, forget about being on any particular rein). When you reach the short side, turn right and, immediately after the corner, turn right again so that you are on a track parallel with the short side. When you reach the side of the arena, turn right and, immediately after the corner, turn right again so that you are now on a line 9m inside the track, parallel to the line you started on. Continue down to the next short side and turn right again, repeating what you did at the top of the school. You can ride this exercise from both directions (see diagrams, above right).

The idea is that you ride all the straight lines, including the ones parallel to the short side, straight, and ride soft curves in each of the corners. In order to ride accurately, you will need to set up the horse for each part – a half-halt before the turn, and applying outside aids as you come onto the straight lines, for instance. You will soon spot your horse's danger areas – the places where he makes life easier for himself by cutting in or falling out. It is up to you to prepare him with half-halts and your inside and outside aids in a way that keeps him consistently to the desired track.

Start this exercise in walk, so that you get the logistics clear in your mind on both reins. When you have mastered it in rising trot, you can start to make some additions – sitting trot on the circles and rising on the long sides.

This exercise really comes into its own in the canter work. Be aware that it is hard work, so change the rein often and fit in some breathers. You can also add a touch of lengthening on the long sides and then extra collection before the corners as an extension of the canter work.

This exercise is useful in a variety of ways. It gives the sharp horse a pattern to adhere to, and so settles him. Lazy horses work harder because of the constant turning. It is also excellent for introducing fittening work into your schooling – especially good for those times when your horse needs to exert himself but the fields are not suitable for cantering.

Because this exercise is hard work, it is worth giving the horse a more active cool down. If you are able to work the horse in a long and low frame, you will find that he will be willing to stretch after the castle exercise. Use the school in a normal way and let him have about five minutes in the new frame, testing changes of bend and half-halts.

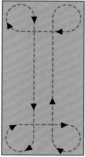

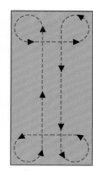

A direction 1   **B** direction 2

COOLING DOWN

1 Make sure you finish every session on a good note.

2 Some riders like to start and finish in a long and low frame. It takes a certain amount of skill to do this in a dynamic way, so have some lessons before attempting it yourself.

3 However, you can help the horse relax in a straightforward way by offering your hands forward and letting the horse stretch down in trot and walk. Make sure your body stays fairly upright – leaning forwards will cause him to lose his balance. If the horse is willing to take the reins in a respectful way, let them slide through your hands, then shorten them a little and let them slide again. Support him with your leg, not to go faster but to maintain the suspension in his stride.

4 I like to give the horse five or 10 minutes' walk on a long rein, preferably out of the school, stretching his head and neck, to let him mentally and physically wind down.

5 Always make sure the horse's breathing is back to normal and any sweat has at least started to dry before taking him back to the stable.

6 If the horse rushes back to the stable, he has not done enough work. Take him back to the arena and work him strongly for ten minutes. Then walk home again on a long rein.

Get results

Want to get more from your schooling sessions? We asked expert trainer Tina Sederholm to devise a range of schooling plans to help you and your horse.

D o you ever wonder what to work on during your flatwork schooling sessions? Perhaps you start out with the best intentions, but find yourself running out of exercise ideas half way through. If so, you are not alone.

It can be difficult to work effectively on your own, without the benefit of an instructor or trainer to suggest helpful exercises and give advice on how to ride them correctly. That's why we have put together a range of schooling sessions designed to work on specific problems you may experience with your horse.

Just follow our schooling session guides and general schooling tips and you should soon see – and feel – the results.

General schooling tips

Spend the first few minutes assessing what frame of mind you and the horse are in today, and how you both feel physically. Spend four or five minutes in walk, trot and canter, while you decide what to work on

Reward your horse when he does well. Give him a pat and let him walk on a long rein for a few minutes. This will allow him to recover physically and rest mentally. It also gives you time to think what to do next

If your arena is not 20m x 40m, make the appropriate adjustments where I have specified measurements

EXERCISES FOR SHARP OR NERVOUS HORSES

Riding a horse on a repeated pattern is a good way to get him to settle. When a horse becomes familiar with the pattern, he will feel more secure and will soon relax. A horse can also feel insecure if he is given unclear instructions about what line he should follow, so part of this exercise is to pay attention to riding accurate diagonals and circles.

Start on the right rein and ride a 20m circle at C. As you go large, ride across

the diagonal from M to K. Then make a 20m circle at A, followed by going across the other diagonal from F to H. This will bring you back to your starting point (see diagram). Repeat the pattern several times in rising trot. You may well notice that your horse starts to fall out and cut in at the same places every time. When you spot theses errors, correct them. The key is to start using the appropriate aids just before your horse goes wrong. In other words, you start thinking ahead of the horse. For instance, your horse may fall out with his outside shoulder as you turn on to the diagonal. This lets you know that

you need to apply your outside aids slightly earlier.

When the horse has settled into this pattern, you can start to add some new elements. Now begin sitting to the trot on the circles, and rising on the diagonals. When you are happy with this, add some lengthened strides on the diagonal. If that works well, or as an alternative, you can strike off to canter at C, make the circle, return to trot at C, go across the diagonal and repeat the same canter work at A.

The exercise is a marvellous introduction to the type of questions you will be asking the horse when you do a dressage test and it increases your awareness of what is happening underneath you. It is also a wonderful tool to use as part of your warm up at a competition, especially if your horse is not listening to you. For example, if he comes out of the lorry fresh and inattentive at a show or event, create an imaginary 40m x 20m arena in the warm-up field, and ride this exercise exactly as you would at home. You will find that, because the horse recognises the routine as one he does regularly, he will soon settle and start listening to you.

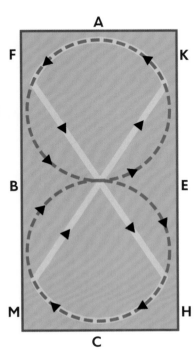

EXERCISES FOR LAZY HORSES

If your horse is a little sluggish or laid back by nature, short bursts of energetic work will really help him.

One way to create more impulsion is to ride 10 strides of working trot rising, followed by five lengthened strides in rising trot, followed by five lengthened strides in sitting trot, immediately followed by a halt. You can keep going with this routine, all around the school, across diagonals, through corners and inside the track.

It is important that you are consistent with the number of strides you take in each phase, so count them out loud to yourself to ensure accuracy. Keep your seat consistent and your hands relaxed as you move from rising to sitting in the trot, as any tension in the hand will inhibit the horse from giving his best.

After a few repetitions of this exercise you will find the horse responds with more power and impulsion. The short bursts of energy improve the activity of the horse's hindlegs and the halt contains that energy before it peters out.

Start your canter work by cantering about half way around the school, turning across the school and making a transition to trot. When you are on the new rein, strike off to canter. Gradually make your turn across the school more acute, and the period of trot shorter, until it becomes a simple change (canter-trot-canter). You can also do canter-walk-canter transitions. When you feel the horse's power has built up underneath you, contrast this work with some gentle loops and circles. The horse will now have more powerful paces, but will also be listening to your forward and controlling aids, so take advantage of this and take good preparatory half-halts before your circles and turns. Rebalancing the horse before a turn or circle enables him to execute the movement easily, and allows you to build up to smaller circles.

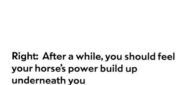

Right: After a while, you should feel your horse's power build up underneath you

Left: Alternating between working trot and lengthened strides will help create impulsion

EXERCISES FOR CHECKING THE BASICS

This is a great all-round exercise for checking up on the basics. It can either be done on the track or, to really test yourself, on a line 3m inside the track.

As you come on to the long side of the arena, bend the horse to the outside for three or four strides, then to the inside for three or four strides. Now ride him straight for six strides, increasing the pace slightly, and then collect him.

As with all these exercises, start in a simple way – say in walk – and only ask for slight bends and changes of pace. You can ask for more as the horse becomes familiar with the exercise. The value in this exercise comes from changing between the different phases, so even if you do not get a wholly satisfactory bend, still move on to the next part of the exercise, but make a mental note to ask the horse in a different way next time. This exercise makes you and the horse flexible and adaptable, in your bodies and your brains.

It is vital that the horse keeps travelling in a straight line during this exercise, so the bend should be primarily in the head and neck. This will make you aware of using your outside aids to control the amount of bend. If you keep looking ahead you will find it easier to maintain the straight line.

Once you have mastered this exercise in walk, do it in trot. When this exercise is done well, it feels as if the horse is dancing. If the horse has a well-established canter, try the following version of the exercise: Ask for outside bend for three strides, ride straight forward in a stronger canter for four strides, then collect him. Using an outside bend in the canter helps get the horse truly straight in his body and encourages him to lift his shoulder, which will add elevation to his canter.

This exercise prepares the horse for practically anything. You can go on and work on some dressage test movements, or start to do some leg yielding. I find it a good way to warm up for jumping, but practise it a few times in a flat-only session first.

Physical education

Need help with schooling sessions to keep your horse's canter together, improve rhythm or make him more supple? Expert trainer Tina Sederholm has devised plans just for you.

EXERCISES FOR KEEPING CANTER TOGETHER

Becoming elongated in the canter is a common problem. The starting point for a manageable canter is to have a neat strike-off where the horse gathers himself and pops into canter. You can work on this with the following exercise.

After the initial warm up, where you should take care to establish a healthy working pace in walk, trot and canter, begin to make some trot-walk-trot transitions. The aim here is to walk for just three or four steps, and maintain a forward-thinking attitude in the horse through the whole procedure.

When you are happy with these, move onto the main exercise. Pick one half of the school to work in. In walk, on the left rein, turn right 2m after the centre line. After about 18m, make a half-circle back to the track. Prepare with a small half-halt and, three quarters of the way through the half-circle, strike off to canter (see the point marked with crossed poles on the diagram). In the middle of the following corner, walk. Then turn up a line 2m after the centre line. Repeat the half-circle and strike off to canter. Halfway through the next corner, walk. Continue on this pattern.

The neat turn will put the horse's hindlegs further underneath him, which will help him make a better strike-off. Cantering for eight to 10 strides only will help maintain the quality of the canter because the horse will not get a chance to become elongated. Take the opportunity to relax your hand at some point during the canter. The confines of this exercise can cause a bit of pressure to build up, so easing off, even just for a second, helps maintain relaxation in the horse.

As soon as you make some progress with this exercise, give the horse a change of scenery. This means giving him some robust trot work around the outside of the school with a light and fun attitude, before returning to the exercise. You may find that the horse is ready to do some good medium trots after this work.

When the horse has done the strike-off exercise well, you can test him out by making a half-halt and striking off to canter on a 20m circle around X. Return to trot after one circle, change the rein and repeat the same canter circle. You want to think quality, not quantity – it's better to do 10 balanced canter strides than a longer distance where the horse's canter deteriorates.

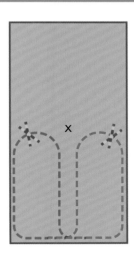

Aim for a forward-thinking attitude from your horse

EXERCISES FOR IMPROVING RHYTHM

Trotting poles are a great way to improve rhythm and add more elevation to the trot. They also test your balance, as you must absorb the increased movement in your horse's back.

Put down three sets of trotting poles – one single pole, one set of three and, for the more experienced horse, one set of five (diagram 1). There should be between 4½'-5' between each pole, adjust this until it's right for your horse. I also build tunnels of poles before and after the trotting poles (see diagram). This helps keep the horse straight and in the centre of the poles.

Start by trotting over the single pole. If your horse is green or spooky, walk over it until he relaxes and accepts it. Some horses will jump the pole the first few times. This is just their natural instinct telling them to avoid something that is on the floor. Pat the horse and ride him over the pole again, keeping him straight and your body balanced and relaxed.

Once the horse has accepted the single pole, move onto the three poles. Be ready to close your leg around him as he makes the extra effort required to negotiate the poles. Keep your balance and keep the horse straight as he makes this effort. Once you are lined up for the poles, focus your attention on a point straight in front of you – a mark on the school wall for instance – and ride towards that. If you need extra assistance, hold onto a neckstrap or a piece of mane.

If the horse jumps the poles, you need to adjust the pace. Try coming a little stronger or slower until you find the optimum tempo. After a couple of good attempts over the poles, start to make loops around them (diagram 2). Change the bend softly so he works other parts of his body.

Then return to the poles and add another dimension to the exercise. After going over in rising trot, sit softly and make a transition to walk or halt as you go through the tunnel. Because the horse has flexed his hindlegs over the poles, the transitions will come easily.

The impulsion created by the trotting poles will carry over to your canter work as well. Work on making small changes of pace in the canter. As you come out of the corner onto the long side, straighten the horse and ask for a stronger canter, thinking upwards and forwards. After four or five strides, collect the horse and soften into a working canter. After some good changes of pace, return to the work over the poles. This time, go over them in sitting trot and, afterwards, go forward into a strong rising trot before collecting in time for the corner.

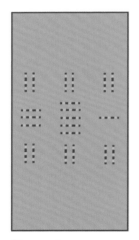
Diagram 1

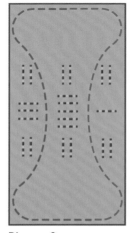
Diagram 2

EXERCISES FOR IMPROVING ELASTICITY

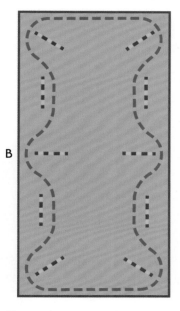

B

Diagram 1

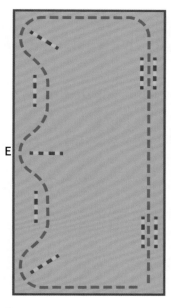

E

Diagram 2

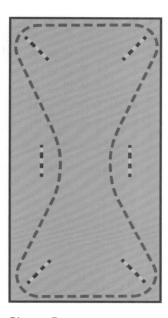

Diagram 3

All horses need to be worked on both sides equally so that they become supple through their bodies. Riders sometimes concentrate too much on the horse's stiff side, but this can be counter-productive as the horse gets tired and becomes even more resistant. To give you an idea of what this feels like, stand on the ground with one arm stretched out horizontally to the side for one minute. You will soon find it gets heavy and tired.

Set the poles out as shown in diagram 1 above. I like to have the poles that point into the corners, and the ones that point inwards at E and B, raised on a block at one end so that it creates a slope to bend around.

After your initial warm up, you can start this exercise in walk. It is your job to guide the horse in and out of the obstacles, changing his bend accordingly. Pick a line that gives you plenty of space around each obstacle (see diagrams for ideas). If the horse clips the end of a pole, you are not paying enough attention to the line that you are supposed to be riding. Make a point of riding straight on the short sides. When the horse is bending

comfortably around the poles on each rein in walk, move into trot.

This exercise is hard work for the horse (and rider) so give him a change by riding some straight lines, either around the outside of the school, or on a track just inside the obstacles.

This exercise is not suitable for canter, so when the horse has done the exercise well in trot, strike off to canter and practise riding a straight line on the inside track. This will be a lot easier than normal, because the bending practice will have made the horse more responsive to your aids.

If you think this is going to be too strenuous for your horse, you can build the bending obstacles on one long side only and, on the other side, build two tunnels inside the track to help you with your straightness (diagram 2).

For the very green or unfit horse, reduce the exercise by just having sloping poles in the corners, and one long pole parallel with E and B (see diagram 3).

Poles raised at one end can be used as obstacles to bend around

On the move

Heather Moffett explains how poor riding can cause a horse to seem lazy and lethargic and how good technique can change his way of going.

We've all heard of riders who are described as having an electric bottom because all the horses they ride seem to speed up when they are on board. Then again, some riders seem to make even fast horses change down a gear.

I often find that lazy, lethargic horses may have a tendency to economy of movement. With correct schooling it is possible to wake them up and transform them into an enjoyable and far more active ride. Unless, that is, the rider is doing something to impede the horse's natural movement.

SITTING TO THE TROT

'Polish the saddle' is a common instruction that always makes me cringe when I hear instructors saying it when teaching sitting trot. Have you ever wondered why some riders, especially dressage riders, appear to flap their legs and nod their head at every stride? Polishing the saddle is the cause.

As one side of the horse's back lowers with each stride, and the rider drives her seat bones forward, the action causes the rider's thighs and knees to drop down together and the lower legs to slip back. As the seat bones then slide forward again, the thighs and knees rise, and the lower legs slip forwards again. Hence the rider's lower legs waggle back and forth involuntarily at every stride.

When the rider is also told to tuck their tail under, any movement through the lower back is blocked, and so it comes out in the neck and shoulders. This is why the head nods up and down involuntarily at each stride.

Viewed from the front, you will clearly see the rider's knees and thighs rising and falling together, rather than unilaterally, and you will notice more movement in the lower leg.

Driving with the seat bones is the root cause of many riding problems

Hands free

Driving with the seat bones is also the cause of the rider's hands chopping up and down. Try this exercise.

Sit on a chair as you would on a horse, with your hands in front of you as if holding the reins. Push both seat bones forwards and back together. Note how your hands rise and fall as you do so. Now imagine you are walking on your seat bones and push one hip forward, then the other. You will find that your hands stay still.

It is almost impossible to drive with the seat and have hands that are independent of the reins. Here is a simple equation that I tell pupils to think about: You have two halves to your backside. The horse has two halves to his back. Put two halves together in sync and you make one. Put two halves together out of sync and you make life difficult for you and the horse.

RIDING AGAINST THE MOVEMENT

The most common cause of a horse's movement being impeded is the rider pushing with her seat. You will often see a rider on a lazy horse trying to urge the horse on by pushing her pelvis forward strongly – rather like a child operating a swing. This actually has the opposite effect on nearly every horse, as it prevents the natural movement in his back.

The horse's back works in two halves, and so should the rider's seat. Thankfully, the Almighty saw fit to design the human rear end in two halves, not only making it easier to walk, but also making it easier to synchronise with the horse!

By pushing both seat bones forward and back at the same time, the rider depresses one side of the horse's back as it rises, and blocks the forward movement of the hindleg on that side. This causes the horse to get slower and, in the case of sensitive, well-trained horses, it will stop them in their tracks. The usual response from the rider is to think that the horse is being lazy and give him a kick or a wallop with the whip, whereas the poor horse is trying to say: "I can't move, you are stopping me with your body."

HOW TO MOVE WITH YOUR HORSE

Allowing your seat bones to rise and fall unilaterally will free your legs to move with the swing of the horse's belly.

For example, the left leg should close lightly as his belly swings to the right, and release as it swings to the left – and vice versa with the right leg. This enables you to use your leg at the optimum time: as the horse's hindleg is off the ground and travelling underneath him.

If you use your leg when the horse's belly is swinging towards it, you will stop the full trajectory of the swing of the ribcage, therefore blocking and shortening the stride.

Using the leg when the belly is swinging away will:

■ Encourage the step under of the hindleg

■ Increase the length of stride

■ Enable the horse's back to swing

The movement your seat bones make when riding correctly in walk mimics exactly the movement they would make if you were walking on foot. One rises as the other lowers, just as the horse's back rises and lowers in two halves. As the hindfoot steps under, the back lowers on that side and your seat bone will lower with it. As the opposite hindfoot steps off the ground, the action will push the back upwards and lift your seat bone up and forward with it.

Allowing your seat bones to rise and fall unilaterally will free your legs to move with the horse's belly

In canter, squeeze and release with your legs once each stride

GET IN THE SWING

Most riders find the unilateral use of the legs difficult to achieve in any pace other than walk, so I advocate using the legs in trot and canter with a quick squeeze and release, once at each stride, in the same rhythm as the trot or canter.

As the action of squeeze and release is fast enough not to impede the swing of the ribcage and belly, I find this works well enough. Walk seems to be the pace that most riders overwork with the legs and seat. This is often in an effort to get the horse to walk out more.

Watch a really good rider from the front (one whose movements appear to blend in unnoticed with those of the horse). You will notice that, in sitting trot, their thighs and knees rise and fall only once at every stride and that, as the horse's back lowers on that side, the lower leg follows the swing of the belly. As the other side lowers, the thigh and knee on that side also lower, and the leg closes

lightly against the belly as it swings away. The legs then remain quiet and still and the rider can clearly feel every movement of the horse's legs underneath.

ABSORBING THE MOVEMENT IN CANTER

Riders are often told to polish the saddle in canter too. In a good canter the horse's back will lift and round, but if the rider is polishing the saddle and driving with the seatbones, her seat will push down heavily against the horse's back and prevent it from lifting, making it flat and hollow.

If the rider merely flexes and straightens her spine in canter, the movement will be absorbed – without any rowing of the shoulders or slipping of the seat on the saddle. This allows the horse's back to round and come up into the rider's seat.

Rise and shine

When ridden effectively, rising trot makes it easy for your horse to use his back naturally and without restriction, says Heather Moffett.

Rising trot is mostly used when warming up, allowing the horse a stretching or rest period in the middle of a schooling session, cooling down, hacking out and when riding a young horse.

If the rider is inadvertently impeding the horse from moving, by the way in which she is rising to the trot, the action of rising becomes meaningless.

In rising trot, the rider is often told that the body should remain upright. I cannot understand the logic behind this. At all other times, except of course when in the forward seat for cross–country or jumping, the upper body should be as still and upright as possible. But in rising trot, the whole idea is to free the horse's back and allow it to work as naturally as possible under us.

PERFECT RISING

Some trainers tell riders to keep the body upright in rising trot. In my opinion this means having to thrust the pelvis furiously forwards and back in order to catch up, or keep up, with the movement of the horse. This is tiring for the rider and it looks like hard work. It is ugly and it causes the horse to rush and flatten.

However, I see plenty of dressage trainers advocating rising like this as it is said to create impulsion. It certainly creates speed if you rise in this manner, but impulsion? I don't think so. I see this as working twice as hard as you need to, and also making the horse have to adjust to your extra movements.

Allowing the pelvis to land slightly tipped forwards means that the buttocks merely touch down and are propelled forwards again by the movement of the horse, not by effort on the part of the rider. In this way, the movement is light and effortless. The rider merely touches down so lightly on the back of the horse that the horse can hardly feel the weight in the saddle. If the buttocks come into full contact with the saddle in the sit phase, the seat will be heavy and limiting for the horse.

The bigger the horse's movement, the more the rider's pelvis will be propelled forwards over the pommel, so that the upper body will be upright in the rise phase of the stride (pic right), but still should return to the saddle with the pelvis slightly forward of the vertical. On a horse with a smaller trot, the pelvis will not be thrown forwards as far by the horse, and so the seat will not leave the saddle very much at all.

It is still essential, however, to allow the pelvis to come sufficiently out of the saddle so that the rider doesn't end up in front of the movement (with the seat back in the saddle before the stride is completed). This is usually caused by the

rider trying to roll the pelvis forwards and back without coming off the saddle at all. This, while probably not causing the horse as much discomfort as coming behind the movement and landing heavily, still shortens the stride and doesn't allow the horse to work in his own rhythm.

FINDING YOUR BALANCE

Using the Equisimulator, I am able to clearly demonstrate the problem without inflicting discomfort on a horse. When I rise to the trot with my body upright, I have to furiously swing my pelvis forwards and back to keep up with the movement. You can see I also ride with my legs pulled forward by the stirrup bar position and have to heave myself up and down in the process, usually with a double bounce. I believe this explains why so many horses experience back problems in the cantle region of the saddle.

When I ride the machine in correct balance, you can see the difference. My upper body is inclined slightly forward, allowing my pelvis to swing lightly forward and back, always landing with the pelvis slightly in advance of the vertical. My rising does not look forced and I am not having to thrust my body forwards to keep up. The landing is light and gentle in the saddle.

RISE TO THE OCCASION

I strongly believe that it is so important to learn to ride well. Not just because it looks better, but because the correct way is the only way in which the horse can work with comparative ease. I am certain that most horses, if given the choice, would choose just to be a horse and eat grass in a field. However, we keep them to ride them. The easier we can make their lives, the happier they are to work with us. I am convinced that remedial trainers and behaviour experts such as Michael Peace would not have nearly as many problem horses to fix if riders paid more attention to how they are riding and listened to their horses, instead of assuming that resistance or evasion is just bad behaviour.

I often think of all the poor horses who are being ridden badly, by riders unknowingly impeding them, and the horse getting a wallop for being lazy when he is trying to say: "I can't go forwards, you are stopping me!" By riding sympathetically and correctly in balance, you can help eliminate many of the problem behaviours riders experience.

STIRRUP BAR

I believe the other cause of the upper body coming too upright in rising trot is the stirrup bar position. I think the design of most saddles makes it difficult for the rider not to land heavily on the cantle region. This is because the stirrup bars on nearly all saddles are too far forwards, causing the rider's seat to be pushed to the rear of the saddle and the thighs to be pulled forwards. This makes the ear/shoulder/hip/heel line difficult to maintain, unless you are a strong and experienced rider, because you are fighting a constant battle with the stirrup leather to stop it swinging forward.

Sit on your saddle and adopt the correct position. Do you find you have to hold the leather back at a 45° angle to maintain the correct line?

If the thigh is pulled forward, the lower leg goes with it and the rider has to pull herself up against the movement. Some riders find it almost impossible to balance in rising trot in a saddle that is forward cut with forward-placed bars. Unless you are riding with very short stirrups and your upper body is well forward, you will not be able to find the point of balance, but will fall back onto the rear of the saddle heavily at each stride.

Using grids

PACE YOURSELF

In-depth advice on grids to help start a novice horse and to slow down a horse who rushes.

I mproving balance, suppleness and obedience are just a few of the benefits you can achieve by working over grids of poles.Using grids regularly as part of your schooling will help you and your horse find jumping easy and fun. Specific grids will also help overcome problems you may be having with your jumping, such as rushing, stopping and knock downs.

F or many years Carol Mailer has been teaching a range of riders from complete beginners to those competing in advanced eventing and show jumping. Carol's speciality is gridwork. She uses grids to enable her to help horse and rider solve their individual problems.

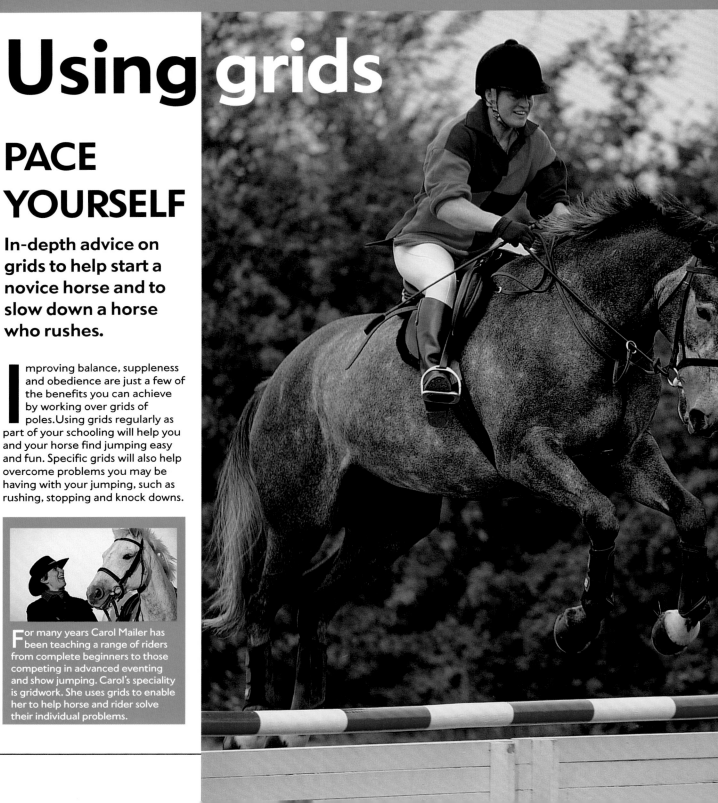

STARTING THE NOVICE HORSE

Before you ask a novice horse to start jumping, he must be able to walk, trot and canter obediently on both reins. Don't even attempt fences until you have this established. Start with five poles on the ground set at 11'-12' apart and approach in trot (grid 1, page184). Even if the horse is suspicious, do not let him turn away. You need to establish, right at the beginning of his jumping career, that there is no option but to go forwards. Continue asking until he goes over the poles, however long it takes. A little patience at this stage will pay dividends later on. Remember to repeat this on both reins. It doesn't matter if he breaks into canter, all you are asking for at this stage is a willingness to get on with it.

When you're happy with his attitude, gradually make the poles into cross fences, starting with the last one (grid 2a, page184) and building backwards until all five poles are altered (grid 2b, page184). Go at a sensible pace and don't rush to get all the poles altered. The cross-poles should encourage the horse to jump in the centre and should be around 1' high to start with. Repeat the exercise on both reins until the horse finds them easy to negotiate without too many rattles. If he stays in trot, don't worry. It is better for him to find the easiest way by repeating the exercise rather than bullying him into canter. Allow the canter to develop naturally, just make sure you ride him forward with enough impulsion to give him confidence.

Everything you attempt at this stage should be small enough for him to step over from a standstill if necessary. Refusals and run outs must be prevented from becoming a habit, so insist on him going through the grid, even if he knocks everything down. If this happens don't worry, just keep repeating the exercise.

When you are totally happy with grid 2b, add a horizontal pole to the last fence, slightly higher than the middle of the cross (grid 3). If you have established his confidence over the smaller poles, this should prove to be no problem for him. If he hesitates or becomes anxious, just go back a step. Repeat the earlier exercises until you feel he is ready to move on without any problems.

Flexible progression is one of the main benefits of starting a novice horse with gridwork. A bolder horse will progress faster than a less confident one, but the end result should be the same. It should only be the timescale that varies, so listen to your horse.

When this exercise is established, progress to grids 4 and 5 (making the middle fences parallels and adding a pole to the first fence). Once your horse is happily jumping this line of poles, try removing the fourth element (grid 6). If all is well, remove the second cross-pole (grid 7). As you can see from the diagrams, you will end up building a small, simple combination.

If your horse starts to get overconfident and hurry, or if he becomes anxious and backs off, go back to jumping the crosses. You need to keep him confident but not cocky. Remember, you are allowing him to learn, not trying too

hard to teach him. Encourage him to work through the grid and manage his own legs. If you overorganise him, he will become too reliant on his rider to get him out of trouble. Concentrate entirely on approaching the grid with impulsion and allow him to choose where his best take-off point will be. Of course he will make mistakes, but let him learn from them. Don't be too tempted to plot his approach with placing poles – he's not going to find them in the ring. Far better to have the grid fences small enough so that any mistakes are not too punishing.

The distances recommended are conventional and are what you would expect to find in doubles or combinations at a novice show. However, the distance of 11'-12' can be shortened if your novice horse finds it difficult. Once the horse has more confidence, gradually increase the distance to 12'. Increase it by inches if necessary. One day he will have to cope with doubles and combinations at a distance of 24'6", so it is as well to try to establish this early.

It would be unwise to lengthen the distance to accommodate a longer stride or bolder horse. A horse with a big stride will need to adjust it to a conventional distance once he starts show jumping. If your horse has a long stride, don't be tempted to remove any cross-poles from the grid until he can cope with grids 2b-5. The crosses will naturally help regulate the slightest hint of acceleration or overlengthening. Take advantage of this, rather than overchecking or fighting with him. When he is more established, you should find him much easier to keep in a rhythm.

Repetition is the key to the harmony and co-operation you are hoping to establish. Don't worry how long it takes, just be patient and be willing to go back a step if it goes wrong.

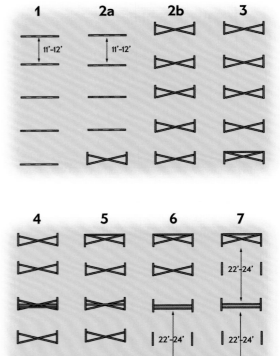

SLOWING DOWN A HORSE WHO RUSHES

If your horse rushes his fences (pics above), use the grid below to establish a good even rhythm and nice rounded jump

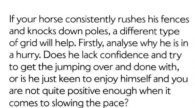

If your horse consistently rushes his fences and knocks down poles, a different type of grid will help. Firstly, analyse why he is in a hurry. Does he lack confidence and try to get the jumping over and done with, or is he just keen to enjoy himself and you are not quite positive enough when it comes to slowing the pace?

Often, the horse develops the habit of rushing purely because the rider turns into a passenger after the fence, allowing the horse to choose his own pace. If you do this, he will soon get the idea of pleasing himself, and it will become a habit that is difficult to break. Whatever the reason, the rider needs to regain the initiative immediately on landing. Steadying on the first stride after the fence will help you approach the next jump with impulsion, rather than speed.

Although the grid below looks a little complicated, try to reproduce it as you'll find it will have a tremendous effect on the way your horse settles and co-operates in his work.

Use the same distances as the novice grid, because you really need to encourage a rushing horse to settle and co-operate on a conventional stride. It can easily be ridden from both reins. Don't forget you will need a helper on the ground to straighten up the poles if they get kicked around. This grid will only be truly effective when set at the correct distances, however tedious it is for the helper!

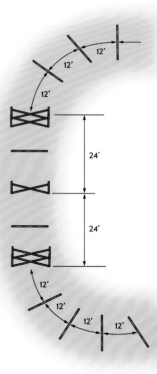

SLOWING DOWN A HORSE WHO RUSHES

When you approach the grid, make sure you come over the curved placing poles in trot. If your horse is in a hurry, approach in walk over the narrower end of the curve.

The first and third cross-poles are parallels. All the crosses should be acute and uninviting, but not too high in the middle – about 2'. The sharper the angle, the more likely the horse is to back off and allow you to use your legs. Unless the horse goes forward from your leg, you will find it impossible to achieve the impulsion required to jump a clear round.

The first parallel cross will be fairly difficult and you should find that you need to actually ride him to the fence instead of hanging on and trying to steady. A high cross-pole produces an optical illusion to most horses and usually encourages them to try to be cleaner and more careful with their jump. A slight suspicion from the horse because the high cross looks unusual may very well work in your favour.

If he jumps the first fence well, but then accelerates through the rest of the grid, be prepared to make the placing poles into high crosses too. As soon as you land over the last fence, make sure you collect up the canter immediately to re-establish his rhythm, balance and, more importantly, pace as you turn away.

The poles at the end will make you aware of how much checking you need to do after a fence. You should be aiming, all the way round the turn, for the poles to fall in the middle of each stride. If they do, you have probably got the balance of pace and impulsion right.

If he is going too fast you will get too close to the take-off spot in front of the pole. If you are not riding him consistently from your leg to hand, you will be too far away. If you can't take charge immediately upon landing, everything will go wrong and you will never negotiate the turn smoothly.

This grid not only helps you to be in a position to encourage your horse to steady, it also affirms when you have got it right. Rushing to the fence can take a long time to correct, as it can soon become a well-established habit. Persistence will pay off in the end, particularly if the grid is set as described. Repetition is the only way to re-establish good habits and co-operation over the speed required to jump easily and cleanly.

The set approach and exit on the grids means that the rider has to be spot on, alert and active and quick to correct any change of pace. You have to give 100% to make sure you remain in charge. The placing and method of negotiating the poles will let you know if you are getting it right, or whether you still need more attention to detail.

Cooling down

Make sure you finish each gridwork session on a good note. Allow your horse to walk on a loose rein for five or 10 minutes after you have finished jumping. Ensure your horse's breathing is back to normal and any sweat has started to dry before taking him back to the yard.

CLEAR ROUND

Working your horse over grids of poles and fences is an excellent way to help improve his balance, suppleness and confidence. These three elements are vital for successful jumping and you will often find that when you establish these, everything else will fall into place. If your show jumping is blighted by knock downs or refusals, the following grids will help you on your way to a clear round.

GRIDS TO HELP FOUR FAULTERS

Firstly, you need to decide what is causing the knock downs. If you don't know, seek some advice from a good jumping trainer. If your horse catches the poles with his front legs, it will probably be your fault. If he is careless behind, you can expect to take most of the blame too! Most horses will jump reasonably accurately, it is usually a case of the rider rushing him or unbalancing him that causes poles to fall.

FRONT LEG RATTLES

A conventional grid (grid 1) can be used to help your horse jump cleanly by adding strategically-placed ground poles. The last fence in this grid is a parallel. If your horse consistently taps poles with his front legs, you have to improve your timing and position to help him be more accurate. Most front leg taps occur because the rider is too keen to approach the fence. You make his job much harder by dropping into jumping position too soon, moving your hand forward and letting your weight swing over the horse's shoulder at the precise moment he wants to lift off. You need to concentrate on riding more positively into a contact and holding it until take-off.

When you have set up grid 1, put a placing pole between each of the fences at the distances shown left (grid 2). This will support the horse and help you to feel the timing required to allow him enough room and time to get his legs out of the way. Note that the poles are not exactly in the middle of the fences. Set them slightly towards the landing side of jumps 1 and 2. This will give you a split second longer to practise not getting in front of the horse's movement.

GRID 1

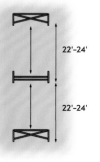

22'–24'

22'–24'

GRID 2

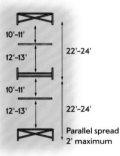

10'–11'
12'–13'   22'–24'
10'–11'
12'–13'   22'–24'

Parallel spread 2' maximum

As you jump, look up and wait for the horse's neck to come to your chest. The placing pole helps round the stride slightly and gives you the elevated feel you need to produce from your leg into your contact (pics above). It will help you recognise that a less keen approach from you will make it easier for your horse. Patience and repetition on both reins is essential. Only by practising will you feel how you should be riding to the jump, rather than looking down and trying to help your horse too much.

The same grid may be used to correct hindleg rattles. Often, it's easy for the rider to slightly misjudge the time the horse is in the air and this can spoil a lovely jump. If you anticipate the landing and start to sit up too soon, you'll put too much weight in the saddle when the horse's hindlegs are still over the poles. Although you may have been in a classic position over the fence, changing your weight prematurely will distract the horse and he will put down too soon, knocking the fence.

Widen the last element of the grid so that the horse has to be in the air a split second longer (maximum 2'). Practise remaining in jumping position, out of the saddle, a second longer so the horse is not distracted into carelessness by your shift in balance. You will be surprised at how much longer you need to hover. Start to readjust your bodyweight as the horse starts to land over the fence. You can see from the picture that this change in timing helps the horse to keep his hindlegs clear of the fence.

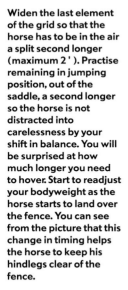 

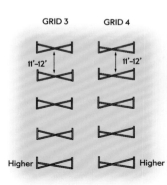

GRID 3   GRID 4

11'-12'   11'-12'

Higher   Higher

Does your horse always seem to dangle one leg more than the other (pic top)? If so, check that you are not causing the problem. It's possible that you might be dropping your shoulder and be crooked yourself, particularly as you approach the end of the grid and anticipate the turn (pic right).

If you are sure you're level over the fences, try this remedy. Build a grid of five bounces using cross-poles 11'-12' apart. Raise the last cross on the side of the habitual dangly leg (grid 3). Change the crosses, one at a time, starting with the final fence and working back (grid 4).

Make sure you stay focused with your steering and ride down the middle of the grid each time.

If you find the raised side is not helping enough, raise it further until the horse has to snap up both legs together. This is a grid that needs to be repeated to be effective, but eventually it will have the desired effect – your horse will become so much more active and accurate.

GRIDWORK TO STOP REFUSALS

If your horse is persistently naughty, nappy and refuses to jump for you, there is a grid that will help you to develop a technique to overcome this. It is essential that you get him checked over by a vet to make sure there is no physical reason for him refusing. Think how difficult it is for you to work with a bad back! If you are certain he is OK and just being awkward, this grid will help.

A spooky approach will lead to a less-than-perfect jump

Build a three-fence grid but make the distances shorter than normal, say 19'-22', and make the last fence a parallel. You need to be sure that your horse isn't stopping because he has to stretch too far to the next fence. Keep the fences small and use plain poles. You will also need a helper.

Approach the grid positively, but not fast. You need to jump with power, not pace. If he stops, don't let him turn away. Either encourage him to jump from a standstill, or dismantle the jump so he can step over it. Do whatever it takes to get over the poles, but try to achieve it by using your legs. It should not be necessary to smack him to make him go. Your leg must be the only aid to send him forward. Using the stick to make him jump is wrong, it gives him completely the wrong signals. Until he goes from your leg, you will achieve nothing.

Give him no option but to go forwards from your leg. Make sure once he starts to co-operate, and he will, that you don't lose the initiative. Keep pushing him into a consistent contact. He will find it easier to do what you want and you will get the feeling of how much leg you need to produce the impulsion for jumping. Stay cool. It gets better the more persistent you are. You should be developing the strength, and more importantly, the attitude necessary to insist on good behaviour.

When he is going freely over the grid, you need to reinforce your wishes when he is asked to do something different. Replace one of the plain placing poles with a very bright one. It will almost certainly guarantee a refusal. Then you can set to work again using the methods you've already established. You know he can jump a pole on the floor, so there should be a distinct lack of sympathy in your attitude to his naughtiness. Once you have him behaving, move the coloured pole. Replace one of the jump poles or put it on the ground instead of a placing pole. Each time he comes to the grid, have the coloured pole in a different place.

Instead of a coloured pole, you could use a plank, anything different will do. The aim of the exercise is to make you positive enough to overcome his tendency to refuse. You will only be strong and positive enough to do this with practice. Only then will you be able to look forward to having some fun.

With practice, your horse will get used to jumping all types of fences

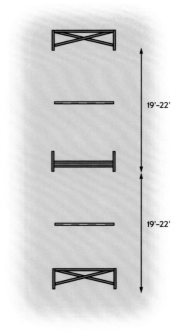

19'-22'

19'-22'

Uprights 1¹/₂-2' high
Parallel spread 2' maximum

Riding Exercises

Tina Sederholm has been involved in training horses and riders from novice to Olympic standard for the last 15 years.

Tina's parents ran an internationally renowned training centre. She has competed regularly at Advanced level – including three-day events such as Blenheim, Bramham and Windsor.

Relaxed jumping

Stay relaxed when you are jumping

The majority of jumping errors are caused by the rider tensing up in front of the fence. The sudden appearance of tension, however small, causes the horse to tighten up and distracts him from the fence, making him much less able to adjust himself. This leads to uncomfortable strides or the horse running out or stopping. Removing this anticipatory tension and replacing it with relaxed confidence is one of the fundamental jobs of any good instructor.

There is a saying that simple awareness is often curative. When you close your eyes you instantly become acutely aware of what is happening via your other senses, and so jumping with your eyes closed is an excellent way to increase your awarenessand sensitivity.

The safest way to try this is in an enclosed area with small fences. Come around the corner into the fence in trot or canter and, once you're on a straight line for the middle of the fence, close your eyes and allow yourself to live with what happens underneath you. Do not close your eyes until you have lined up for the fence. If you feel the horse drift to the left or right you can correct that, and if you feel the necessity to close your legs to support your horse into the fence, do so. Do as little as possible apart from maintaining your softness and balance, and open your eyes on landing.

If you stay relaxed and follow the motion of the horse, you will feel him adjusting his stride and will be able to stay with him. However, if you make a jerky move, you will get a jerky result. It is important that you do not take a sneaky peek because it will make you indecisive and produce another wobbly jump.

As an alternative, you can use counting to create a relaxed but alert approach. The key is to count every stride out loud, keeping your voice calm and even. When your voice stays relaxed, so does your body. If your voice speeds up or gets squeaky, it shows tension has come into your body.

Don't close your eyes until you have lined up for the fence

These exercises are designed to assist you in staying relaxed in front of the fence. The more relaxed you are the more easily the horse can adjust himself, and his confidence in you will grow if you allow him to do this in an uncomplicated way.

If you are relaxed in front of the fence, your horse will be able to jump smoothly and softly in rhythm

Crossed reins

Even out imbalance in your hands

Most of us, whether we admit it or not, favour one side of our body, and this often emerges when we are riding as being stronger with one hand than the other. One way to even out this imbalance is to ride with your reins crossed.

You will soon identify which side is the stronger because, if you use just one hand, the horse immediately moves in the opposite direction to the one you are expecting.

Try doing all your normal work – circles, straight lines and transitions with crossed reins. What is interesting about this exercise is that, although it involves your reins, it actually takes the emphasis off using your hands to get what you want from the horse. You have to ride the horse primarily with your seat and legs and use your hands in conjunction with each other, rather than relying on the reins alone for steering.

Also, if you want to put the horse on the bit, you will find that you really have to ride the horse up to the hand, because it is almost impossible to pull down and back, a cover-up technique some riders use for keeping their horses in an outline.

If you have stiff arms this exercise will help you become more flexible, as this position allows your arms to work around your body in a fluid way, especially when it comes to riding transitions.

Like most unfamiliar situations, riders are often resistant to this exercise, but the benefits outweigh the initial discomfort. You may even come to love it. One of my father's pupils, a former Badminton winner, used to ride his show jumping rounds with crossed reins because of the way it evened out him and his horses.

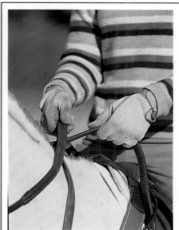

How to do it
Cross your reins – hold the left rein in your right hand and the right rein in your left hand. Hold them as if you were driving – with the rein lying over your first finger and your thumb on top (pic above).

Where you look is where you go

Look where you are going when you're jumping

One of the best ways to keep your concentration and react 'in the moment' when you are jumping is to consistently look where you are going.

In this particular exercise you jump on a 20 to 30m circle. Place a jump on the centre line of the arena (on one edge of the circle) and build a tunnel of poles directly opposite (the other side of the circle). I like to have the middle pair parallel with the jump wings and a pair set at an angle either side, to encourage you to ride a well-shaped circle.

The idea of this exercise is to continually move your attention to the next quarter of the circle. If you are coming out of the tunnel you look at the approach to the fence. As you come into the approach you look at the fence, and so on.

The best way to do this is to have a friend in the middle of the circle asking you, "What are you looking at?" To which you reply out loud "at the fence, at the landing," and so on. Because you are focusing on a specific point, your body automatically co-operates to get you there.

You will soon find out where you lose attention. For most people that is directly after the fence. The result is they often miss their turn into the tunnel. It is equally important to have your attention on where you are going in this area too, because if you are disorganised here it will affect your approach into the next fence.

It is best to start this exercise with a pole on the ground so you get your line right before starting to jump. Make sure too that you only jump two or three times and then have a break before approaching on the other rein. This exercise is hard work for the horse. Plus, you need time to assess where you keep your attention and the places where you lose it, so that your next turn is an improvement.

Bends and turns

Establish bend in your horse

There are lots of ways to bend a horse. You can decide to bend just his head and neck or, more commonly, ask him to bend through his whole body in the shape of a crescent. Also, he needs to be able to bend in order to turn. Riders often get in a muddle about what they are asking for, and end up giving half-hearted messages.

I like to think about the shape I want to create in the horse, and which direction I want his body to go in. Then it becomes more obvious where and how much to use the hands and legs. If you want the horse to bend to the inside, on a circle for example, move your hands as a pair to the outside of the bend, while deepening your inside heel to get that 'give' in the horse's side. If the horse is a little resistant to this in his jaw, vibrate the inside rein. Your outside leg should be placed slightly behind the girth so that the crescent-shaped curve is completed behind the saddle. The amount of bend you have is determined by how far out you take your outside hand, but the inside hand must not go across the withers.

Set up markers on a straight line. Bending in and out of these will make you familiar with changing your aids, train your co-ordination and stop you concentrating too much on one side of your horse.

Remember, these aids are just to bend the horse. Once bend is established, you will need to use turning aids to ride correctly through a corner, or turn down a centre line.

Smooth transitions

Achieve smooth, light transitions

Some horses can be quite strong in transitions and pull the rider out of the saddle. It is then easy to pull back and get into a tug of war with the horse. One way to break this cycle is to make transitions holding onto a neck strap.

Hold your reins normally and place both hands on a neck strap. The neck strap can be an old stirrup leather or the neck piece of a martingale. If you have short arms, you may need to make the neck strap a little looser than I have in the photograph, but beware of having it too loose, because it will not be so effective.

Start in walk and ask for a transition to halt. As you do so, close your hands on the neck strap so it presses on the underside of the horse's neck. As soon as he responds, release your hand to release the pressure of the neck strap on his neck. This is the reward to the horse. Rewards are a major key to training horses, so it is a good idea to train yourself to give them in an obvious way.

Make sure you also have a contact with the horse's mouth when you make these transitions, as he will then start to associate light pressure on his mouth with changing pace. However, because you have the added signal from the neck strap, it will not turn into a battle of strength.

This exercise also gives the rider greater security in the transition. It's easy to wobble about in transitions or tighten up because you anticipate discomfort. The security that the neck strap gives you will allow you to relax in your seat and accept the change of pace, rather than bracing yourself against it.

Once the walk-to-halt transition is working well, you can try the same thing in trot and work on the transition to walk, and so on. It is worthwhile keeping your hands on the neck strap all the time, even in between practising transitions. Doing this will encourage a soft, consistent contact with the bit and, as the horse starts to give in his jaw in the transitions and you ride forward into them, he may well start to go on the bit.

Ride like a jockey

Improve your balance and position

A good way to achieve an independent and well-balanced position is to stand up in trot with short stirrups and bridged reins. You can do this during your fittening work or in the school. Standing up with short stirrups in trot makes you extremely aware of your balance, and you'll soon find that the easiest way to maintain your balance is to keep your lower leg at the girth. Allowing the lower leg to fly back will cause you to lose your balance and rely on the reins for support. In order for this exercise to work, the horse must be going genuinely forward.

You can continue to train your balance by cantering with very short stirrups, during which you also get a sense of what it is like to be still on top of the horse and let him move underneath you. This is excellent for anybody who is intending to ride cross country.

Riding like this can give the rider the feeling of the horse being truly 'together' in an uncomplicated way, as well as strengthening those leg muscles and increasing flexibility. It is hard work, but it is well worth it, and makes riding in normal length stirrups seem really easy! When you are confident with your balance in this exercise, you can also work on the horse. While you are standing up, close the hands around the reins for a few strides and then release, close and release. If this is done with a sensitive hand and the horse is given a little time to become used to it, he will give in his jaw. When his jaw gives in this way and he responds to the closing hand, he will also collect himself nicely.

The advantage here is that the horse becomes mentally obedient and, because you are standing in the stirrups, he will have space for his back to round and he will be able to bring his hindlegs underneath him. Practise this a few times and his back will become soft and flexible and will be a pleasure to sit on.

Sort out your canter strike-offs

Improve your canter strike-off

A neat strike-off is the foundation for a well-balanced canter. A messy strike-off, when the horse rushes from trot into an elongated canter, is difficult to recover from. These rough transitions are sometimes due to rider error and sometimes the horse is confused. Here are two exercises to help. Apart from giving the horses clear aids, the most important factor in a good strike-off is that you keep your balance at the crucial moment of transition. Many riders, in the desire to get into canter, lean forward to urge the horse on and load his shoulder, just at the moment that the horse wants to be lifting it in order to jump into canter.

A simple remedy for this is to turn your head and look to the outside at the same time as you apply the aids for canter. It is best to do this in the corner of the school, because you then have something specific to focus on. Looking to the outside centralises the upper body and allows your inside hip to come forward just as the horse lifts his inside hip – the action he needs to do in order to strike off. This exercise is particularly good if the horse persistently strikes off on the wrong leg, a mistake that is nearly always due to rider error.

This action also counteracts the habit of having a sneaky look down to check if the horse is on the correct lead. Instead, you will feel the strike-off through your seatbones and it will become a calmer and more elegant experience.

If your horse is confused about the strike-off, you can use another exercise to clarify the transition. Place two poles in a funnel shape, about 6m apart at the narrow end, and 12m apart at the wide end. On the left rein, trot around the end of one pole and go through the middle of the funnel. Change your bend to the right, turn right as you go through the narrow part and strike-off to right canter.

The shift of weight caused by the change of bend will position the horse so that he finds it easy to canter, and the poles will help you pick a neat line. Remember, if your horse struggles in the canter, just try for short periods – maybe 10 or 12 strides – before coming back to trot or walk, and repeating the exercise in the opposite direction.

Let your horse do his job

Improve your approach to a fence

Watch any horse loose jump, and you will probably see him making some clever adjustments into the fence. However, when we put a rider on board who anticipates the fence, the resulting tension shoots rigidity into the horse, preventing him from adjusting or, worse still, pushing him blindly into the obstacle.

The ability to stay relaxed yet alert on the approach to a fence is one of the fundamental qualities of a good show jumping rider. One way to train this is to look away from the fence on the approach. Once you have lined up for the fence, fix your eyes onto an object, or better still a person standing to the side of the fence, about 5m before it. It is important not to sneak a quick glance at the fence as this negates the exercise.

To make the exercise more fun, and ensure you keep your attention on the person, ask them to hold up some fingers as you approach them. You can then say out loud the number of fingers they are holding up as you approach.

With these distractions in place, you will keep your body relaxed, therefore following the horse smoothly and absorbing any adjustments he makes.

Start with small fences to build up your confidence and prepare to be delighted with the harmonious approaches you and your horse achieve.

Sitting comfortably

Improve your sitting trot

Sometimes, when I mention the words 'sitting trot', I am met with groans and scrunched up faces. However, when you have mastered sitting trot, it's one of the most wonderful ways to feel connected with your horse and feel what is going on underneath you. In addition, it is a must if you want to progress from basic flatwork.

The root of good sitting trot lies in a level pelvis and moveable hip joints. The hip is a ball and socket joint capable of a great range of movement – think how a ballerina can make graceful circles and arcs with her leg – and the mobility we have here allows us the extra room we need to accommodate the horse's back. However, if you attempt sitting trot with stiff hip joints, you will end up bouncing against the saddle, quickly followed by tension as you brace yourself against the pain.

The first way to improve your sitting trot is to mobilise the hip. Locate your hip joint by placing your fingers on the outside of your thigh (main pic), and moving your leg backwards a little so you can feel the hip joint working. When you have located it, put your palm flat against your thigh with the inside of your wrist pressed against the piece of bone that is sticking out (inset pic). Gently lift your leg away from the saddle and rotate it backwards.

If you are very stiff, you may need a friend to lift your leg away for you so that you get the feeling of doing it in a soft way. If you find yourself using lots of effort, relax and make the movement smaller.

When you feel a difference, stop the exercise, walk on and go into sitting trot. Trot for a few strides, keep breathing and think of keeping your hips as fluid as possible. Go for quality, not quantity. Then halt, repeat the mobilising exercise and try a few more strides of sitting trot. Repeat this exercise every few days.

Perfect your sitting trot

Following the motion of your horse

This exercise will help to level out your pelvis, give you the feeling of following the motion of the horse and encourage the self-carriage necessary for really good sitting trot.

This sequence starts with the exercise 'legs away'. Keep your body vertical and lift both legs, from the hips, away from the sides of the horse. Hold this position for a couple of seconds and then replace them softly around the horse. The key is to think of "lifting your bones" rather than use any sort of momentum to throw your legs away from the sides of the saddle.

When you are familiar with this exercise, you can add the next element. Holding the reins in one hand, circle one arm backwards.

When your arm is adjacent to your ear (pic 1), hold it still and straight and take your legs away for a couple of strides. Then let the legs come back down, and complete the circle with your arm. You can repeat the exercise with the other arm.

The arm that is held straight up in the air will help your body lengthen and stay tall, while taking your legs away in walk will allow your seat to naturally follow the movement of the horse.

After you have co-ordinated these two actions, you can incorporate a third. When your arm is stretched up, turn your head so you are looking in the opposite direction (pic 2) and then take your legs away. Finish by letting your legs down, looking straight in front of you and completing the circle.

After practising this a few times, hold the reins normally and try some sitting trot. Done correctly, the legs away will have levelled out your pelvis, and the straight arm will have improved your self-carriage, making sitting trot a more enjoyable experience for you and your horse.

If you want to do this exercise in trot and canter, it is best to do so on the lunge, so that someone else has control over the horse and you can use your spare hand to hold the front of the saddle.

Balance and flexibility

Improve your balance and flexibility

Good balance is reliant on flexible joints, just like the suspension on your car. Your joints act as shock absorbers, accommodating the action of the horse. Working with short stirrups is a great way to work on your balance and make sure that you are able to use your joints effectively.

When working with short stirrups, use a 'two point' or jumping position (pictured below). It's easiest to use this position in trot and canter, when you have some motion underneath you – after all, it is a close relation of the position you would assume when riding at higher speeds.

Practise this position a few times in halt to get the logistics of the position correct to start with.

Like a sturdy tree, a good seat needs a sound root and in the jumping position, that root is the position of your lower leg. Your stirrup leather should hang vertically so that the ball of your foot in the stirrup is parallel to the girth with your weight going down through your calf and heel. There should be equal flexion in your hip, knee and ankle joints. Your body weight is distributed evenly over your lower leg, with your seat out of the saddle, and your upper body inclined slightly forward. Your hands rest on the neck, but they are mainly there as a point of contact and should not be leant on in any way.

Once you find your balance in jumping position, hold it for a few seconds, and come down softly into the centre of the saddle. Bring your upper body upright and your pelvis forward as you bring your bottom down, so that you end up sitting vertically, in the deepest part of the saddle.

You can test your balance in the jumping position in trot in another way. When you have established your position, put the reins in one hand resting on the neck and put the other hand on your hip. After a few strides, change hands. Repeat this exercise until you find it easy to change hands.

If you are feeling adventurous, you can try in canter too. If the horse shoots off while you are changing hands, this is feedback that you are not maintaining your balance. Make sure you regularly come back to rising trot or sitting in the canter – as the change between the two positions does you as much good as the jumping position itself.

Muscles need to contract and expand to maintain their elasticity, so even if your focus is primarily dressage, shortening up your stirrups occasionally acts as a useful strengthening exercise. Generally I find that once riders have ridden with shorter stirrups, they are able to find greater depth when they let their stirrups down again.

Achieving a good contact

Develop sensitive and effective rein aids

Keeping a consistent contact with your horse's mouth is an important factor in enabling good communication between you and your horse. The aim is to have hands which are reliable and sensitive and move when you decide you want them to!

One way to create this consistency of contact is to ride holding a stick in front of you. The best device to use is the end of a slim broom handle, but anything that is easy to hold and does not bend will work.

The stick will help you to keep your hands level and carried. It gives your contact an all-round feel, rather than being separated into left and right rein. It is especially helpful when riding through turns, because you will get the feel of exactly how much to give the outside rein, while maintaining a contact.

The stick has a myriad of other positive effects; it helps stabilise the rider during transitions, and encourages the rider to sit level. Because your hands are on the same plane, your elbows and shoulders become level and so on – it has a domino effect through your whole body.

The stick acts like training wheels on a bicycle – it gives you stability. Once you have experienced this, you can take the stick away and you will know the feel you are looking for.

This exercise is a useful addition to any rider's or instructor's toolbox. When words and theoretical understanding are not enough to result in a change, the stick will often do the trick.

Getting your horse on the bit

First step to getting your horse on the bit

Most riders want, at some stage, to learn how to put the horse on the bit. However, it does seem to be one of the areas where the most confusion and misunderstanding occurs between horse and rider.

I think one of the contradictions of putting the horse on the bit is that he is supposed to give in his jaw and, at the same time, take a contact.

In my opinion, the feel you are looking for could be described as the horse feeling spongy and relaxed in his jaw. You feel this sensation through the rein, into your hand. When he is truly connected up to the bridle he will also feel light, but this quality comes from him carrying himself well, not a feeling that he hardly dare touch the bit.

My solution to achieving this spongy feel is this: In halt, put the reins in one hand, with one rein overlapping the other within your fist. Put your hand on the horse's neck with your knuckles pressing into the mane. If necessary, shorten your reins so that you maintain a contact.

The horse will almost definitely stiffen his jaw against this, so, while keeping your hand in the same place, gently vibrate your fingers until he gives in the mouth. Don't worry if he moves backwards or is a little awkward, just let your hand stay settled.

The moment he gives, move your hand forward a couple of millimetres, as a reward. This is a small movement because you do not want to lose the contact – just let him know he has done the right thing. You can use the same technique in walk and trot. If the horse resists in a major way, go back and do the exercise in halt.

After a few minutes, put the reins in both hands and maintain the same quality of contact, and enjoy the feel of an accepting jaw.

Take your own line

Riding a correct line

Do you ride the line you have chosen, or do you let your horse decide? Riding in an arena can lull you into thinking that you are directing the horse, when often the horse is just following the well-trodden furrow of the outside track.

One way to test that you are the one deciding which track the horse takes is to ride a line 5m inside the track on the long sides of the school. Horses get security from walls and fences and will lean towards them. In order to ride straight, you need to make an active effort to do so, rather than turning and hoping everything will be all right. Pick a point at the end of the school and ride positively forward towards it. Imagine you are riding your horse along a railway track and that you are trying to keep him within the metal rails.

Your horse may try to drift back to the track, especially if he is used to going around the outside of the school. For example if, on the right rein, he falls out with his left shoulder and drifts to the left, you need to use your left leg and rein to counteract this. Close and release your hand and leg several times while, at the same time, holding open your right rein to encourage the horse in that direction. Keep your eyes on your chosen point. This also works well when riding down the centre line, where you can focus on the markers at C or A.

Remember also to give your horse specific instructions when you want him to turn. If you do nothing, you will feel the horse wobbling underneath you, trying to guess what he should do. Keep riding straight and, when it is time to turn, look where you want to go, and then apply your turning aids.

You can also try the following technique to improve your straightness. Pick a marker on the opposite side of the school, look at it and say out loud, for example, "I am riding to B." As you arrive at B, say your next move out loud, "At C, I am turning up the centre line." Continue like this for a few minutes and you will find that not only are your lines better, but that you become more aware of the quality of your horse's rhythm.

Training yourself to maintain a line in this way will pay off when you come to ride outside, or in a dressage arena that has only low boards to keep you in.

Switch between riding off the track and riding on it. When you are on the track, make sure you pay just as much attention to giving the horse clear directions. Clear, consistent directions will help make the horse feel secure, and the more secure he feels, the more he will give himself to you. Eventually, this improved security will lead to an attentive and responsive horse and your partnership will grow.

Riding a round circle

Preventing your horse falling out or cutting in

How often do you find yourself riding an egg-shaped circle? Are you aware what shape your circle is at all?

I often find that riders get so preoccupied with an inside bend, or getting the horse on the bit, they forget to ride a correct circle. The irony is that when you pay attention to the line you are riding, the bend often sorts itself out, and the horse relaxes and softens because he is getting clear instructions from you.

This idea follows on from the importance of riding your own line. The same principle of becoming the architect of what is happening underneath you,

rather than assuming what is taking place, can be applied to improving your circles.

I can almost guarantee that if a horse cuts in on one part of the circle, he will fall out in the area that is directly opposite. Riders sometimes misinterpret this as, "He's resisting, resisting...oh good, now he's given," but in reality the horse is just resisting you in a different way by escaping through the outside shoulder.

Luckily, you can use the fact that horses are creatures of habit, and will keep repeating the same behaviour until you correct it, to your advantage. As the horse will keep cutting in and falling out in the

same place until you do something about it, you can catch the error before it happens.

It is a good discipline to ride circles that are completely inside the outside track of the school so that you can observe what is happening. If, for example, the horse starts to fall out as you come parallel to the entrance of the school, next time around start to apply your outside aids 3–4m before the point at which he started to lose his shoulder and fall out.

It is vital that you apply the outside aids before he starts to fall out, otherwise the old habit will still be present and you will simply be limiting the damage rather than teaching your horse something positive.

Once you have successfully corrected one side of the circle, observe what is happening on the opposite side. The circle may already be evening out because of the work you have done, but it is more likely that you will need to apply inside aids and lead out with the outside hand (an open rein) to correct the cutting in.

Falling out is a sign of resistance

Whether you are using increased inside or outside leg, make sure you gently massage the horse with a leg that squeezes and relaxes, rather than one that is clamped on. If you clamp the leg on it becomes stiff and will feel like an iron rod to the horse, which is hardly something he will want to 'give' to.

Practise riding circles of varying sizes, taking into account your horse's fitness and level of schooling, and make sure you have decided what size your circle is going to be before you execute it. This way, you will have a much better chance of riding a beautiful round one.

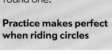

Practice makes perfect when riding circles

Riding past a spooky object

How to ride safely past a scary object

Have you ever noticed how your horse sees things that you do not? You can be hacking down the road and, for no apparent reason, he leaps out from underneath you. Horses are flight animals, and it's part of their natural instinct to be on the lookout for danger.

Despite domestication, this instinct stays with them, just as when you hear a loud bang it makes you jump. However, when a horse leaps out of the way, the rider often punishes him, which only confirms to the horse that he is in a serious position. This does nothing to help the situation; in fact it can heighten his spookiness and make him even more wary.

The key to this situation is to pay attention yourself. You will notice that before the horse spooks, he gives you a warning signal that something is wrong. You need to tune into your horse to be able to spot the sign, as it may be quite small. He might prick his ears more sharply or tighten in his neck. This is your signal to respond and put his focus elsewhere before he has the time to

jump sideways.

You can do a lot to influence your horse's state of mind by dealing with your own. If you tighten up, the horse will too. The first step is to be aware of when you do this, and do something different. You need to remain as calm as you can, and

you can achieve this is by keeping your breath regular. It's easy to pre-empt the horse's spook by holding your breath, sending a message that says, "Danger ahead!" Instead, keep breathing and look in another direction, preferably the one in which you want to go.

If your horse spooks in the school, try this exercise. Pick a line far enough away from the troublesome object that he is not going to have a big reaction. Trot past the object with the horse's head and your attention turned away from it. The idea is to get the horse's body closer to the object without forcing him to look at it. When the horse has gone past, give him a pat. Next time pick a line a couple of metres closer, and the next time get closer still. Each time, pat him to reassure him that he has done well to go past. If he reacts, go back to a line further away.

Soon the horse will relax and accept whatever is frightening him. Now you have a horse who is mentally ready to start work but, like all training, this requires patience. A few minutes spent acclimatising your horse to spooky objects before you start schooling will prevent the whole session turning into an argument later on.